The Overloaded Ark

And they went in unto Noah into the ark, two and two of all flesh, wherein is the breath of life.

(Gen. VII, xv)

ff

GERALD DURRELL

The Overloaded Ark

faber and faber

LONDON · BOSTON

First published in 1953
by Faber and Faber Limited
3 Queen Square, London WC1N 3AU
First published in this edition 1963
Reprinted 1965, 1967, 1969, 1971, 1974, 1978
and 1987 (twice)
Printed in Great Britain by
Redwood Burn Ltd Trowbridge Wiltshire
All rights reserved

ISBN 0 571 05371 8

Contents

Illustrations

ILLUSTRATIONS

Author's Acknowledgements

Both John Yealland and I would like to thank the following people, who, while we were in the Cameroons, helped and advised us in many ways.

Of the United Africa Company: Mr. Baker and Mr. Milsome of Mamfe, and Mr. Coon at Victoria, who dealt with the many problems of supplies and transport.

The Elders and Fyffes representatives at both Victoria and Tiko who helped us to secure return passages for ourselves and our animals, and the Captain and crew of the ship we travelled back on, who did their utmost to make our voyage easy.

To the various District Officers in the Cameroons who helped us in many ways, and in particular, Mr. Robins, District Officer for the Mamfe Division, who did much to smooth our difficulties for us.

We are deeply indebted to the Reverend Paul Schibler and his wife, of the Basle Mission in Kumba, who perhaps did more than anyone else in helping us in our work when we stayed with them at Kumba.

We would also like to thank all those Africans—personal staff, hunters, guides and carriers—without whose work and help we should have achieved very little.

Finally, I would like to thank Miss Sabine Baur for the trouble and care she has taken over the illustrations for this book, and my wife, who helped in the preparation of the manuscript and who bravely undertook the dangerous task of criticizing my work.

ARTIST'S ACKNOWLEDGEMENTS

I must first of all thank Mr. Durrell for his very helpful sketches and photographs.

Dr. L. Forcart and Dr. E. Sutter, members of the staff of the Museum of Natural History of Basle, very kindly sought out much useful material for me; and I am particularly indebted to Dr. A. Portmann for his criticisms and suggestions and for his most valuable help in producing the necessary documents for my drawings.

The drawing on the title page is adapted from a painting by the American artist E. Cheverlange.

A Word in Advance

★

This is the chronicle of a six months' collecting trip that my companion and myself made to the great rain forests of the Cameroons, in West Africa. Our reasons for going on this trip were twofold: firstly, we wanted to collect and bring back alive some of the fascinating animals, birds, and reptiles that inhabit this region; secondly, we had both long cherished a dream to see Africa: not the white man's Africa, with its macadam roads, its cocktail bars, its express trains roaring through a landscape denuded of its flora and fauna by the beneficial influences of civilization. We wanted to see one of those few remaining parts of the continent that had escaped this fate and remained more or less as it was when Africa was first discovered.

This was to be our first collecting trip. John Yealland's interest lay with birds, while mine lay with mammals and reptiles. Together we had planned and financed the trip; for a venture such as this you need a great deal of capital, as you are not financed by the zoos you collect for. However, they help you in every way they can, and supply you with lists of the specimens they would like from the area you are going to, so you know before you start which animals you particularly want.

There has been quite a bit written about the collecting of wild animals, and most of it gives a very untrue picture. You do not spend your time on a trip risking death twenty times a day from hostile tribes or savage animals; on the other hand you do not sit in a chair all day and let the "blacks" do all the work for you. Naturally, doing this sort of work, you are bound to run certain risks, but they have been greatly exaggerated: nine times out of ten any dangers you encounter are of your own making. Without the help of the natives you would stand little chance of catching the animals you want, for they know the forest, having been born in it; once the animal is caught, however, it is your job to keep it alive and well. If you left this part of it to the natives you would get precious little back alive. Ninety per cent of your time is spent tending your captures, and the rest of your time in tramping miles through the forest in pursuit of some creature that refuses to be caught. But in writing a book about a collecting trip you naturally tend to stress the highlights rather than the dull routine work. After all, you don't want to write two hundred and fifty pages on how you cleaned out monkey cages, or cured diarrhoea, or any one of the odd things you had to do every day. So, if the following pages contain mainly descriptions of the more interesting adventures we had, it does not mean to say that there were not the dull and unpleasant periods, when the world seemed to be full of uncleaned cages or sick specimens, and you wondered why you ever came on the trip at all.

Finally, I would like to exonerate my companion from any blame in foisting this history upon the public. Having suffered much at my hands in the tropics he now has to suffer once more in print; that he will do this with his usual placidity, I have no doubt. But I would like to place it on record that when I told him I was writing a book about our trip he made the following statement: "Take my advice, old boy," he said earnestly, "and don't. . . ."

Prelude

The ship nosed its way through the morning mist, across a sea as smooth as milk. A faint and exciting smell came to us from the invisible shore, the smell of flowers, damp vegetation, palm oil, and a thousand other intoxicating scents drawn up from the earth by the rising sun, a pale, moist-looking nimbus of light seen dimly through the mists. As it rose higher and higher, the heat of its rays penetrated and loosened the hold the mist had on land and sea. Slowly it was drawn up towards the sky in long lethargically coiling columns, and gradually the bay and the coastline came into view and gave me my first glimpse of Africa.

Across the glittering waters were scattered a handful of tiny islands, each a cone-shaped mass of vegetation, so overloaded that it seemed they must topple into the waters under the weight of this climbing tower of leaves. Behind them the coastlands climbed upwards, covered with a thick, unbroken quilt of trees, to where, dim and gigantic, Mount Cameroon crouched, gilded by the morning light. The colours of this landscape, after the pale pastel shades of England, seemed over bright, almost garish, hurting the eyes with their fierce intensity. Over the islands flocks of grey parrots wheeled in strong, rapid flight, and faintly their clownish screams and whistles came to us. In the glistening wake of the ship two brown kites circled in an anxious search for something edible, and out of the remaining skeins of mist being drawn up into the sky, a fishing eagle suddenly appeared, heavy and grace-ful, its black and white plumage shining. Over all this, the land and sea seen obscurely through the shifting, coiling mist, lay the magic smell we had noticed before, but now it was stronger, richer, intoxicating with its promise of deep forest, of lush reedy swamps, and wide magical rivers under a canopy of trees.

We landed as in a dream, and were rudely brought back to earth by a nerve-shattering half-hour with the Customs, try-ing to explain our eccentric baggage. At last we were speed-ing along the road to Victoria, a red earth road lined with hibiscus hedges aflame with flower, and copses of the yellow, feathery, pungent-smelling mimosa. We arrived at the little white rest house on the hill where we were to live for a week, and proceeded to look around. We had much to do, and in any other place it would probably have seemed irksome; as it was we were interviewed, our numerous papers stamped, we purchased vast quantities of stores, went to dinner with numbers of kind people, swam in the sea, and did a great many other things in a sort of dream-like trance. Every-where we went there was something new to see. The strag-gling town lay along the side of the bay, filled with rustling palms, hibiscus and bougainvillæa hedges glowing with flowers, and in every compound and garden stood sedate rows of canna lilies, like vivid flames on thin green candle-sticks. It was an enchanting place, but even so we yearned for the day when we should move up country. At last it dawned.

The lorry had been ordered to arrive at the rest house at seven-thirty for loading, and by eight-thirty we thought we should be well on the road. It was very apparent that we were new to Africa. At ten o'clock we were pacing round and round our mountain of luggage on the veranda, cursing and fuming impotently, scanning the road for the truant lorry. At eleven o'clock a cloud of dust appeared on the horizon and in its midst, like a beetle in a whirlwind, was the lorry. It screeched to a halt below, and the driver dismounted. I noticed an assortment of odd passengers sitting in the back, about twelve of them, chatting happily to each other with their goats, chickens, bags of yams, calabashes of palm wine, and other necessities of travel spread out around them in the lorry. I stormed down to interview the driver, and it was then I learned that it is better not to inquire why a lorry is late in the Cameroons: I was treated to at least six different and contradictory reasons, none of which satisfied anyone except the driver. Wisely leaving this subject, I turned my attention to the crowd in the back of the vehicle. It transpired that this was the driver's wife, this was the driver's wife's cousin, this was the father of the motor-boy, and this was the motor-boy's mother-in-law, and so on. After a prolonged altercation which for shrillness and incomprehensibility could not have been rivalled by any race on earth, they were removed, together with their household goods and livestock. The driver then had to turn the lorry for loading, and my faith in his abilities was rudely shattered when he backed twice into the hibiscus hedge, and once into the rest house wall. Our baggage was then loaded with a speed and lack of care that was frightening, and, as I watched, I wondered how much of our equipment would be left intact on arrival in Mamfe. I need not have worried. It turned out later that only the most indispensable and irreplaceable things got broken.

During my tête-à-tête with the driver, and my careful genealogical investigation of the passengers, John had taken no part. Now, as the pandemonium lessened, he wandered round the front of the lorry and discovered something that amused him greatly. Above the windscreen, in large white uneven letters, had been printed "THE GODSPEED . . . VICTORIA TO KUMBA". That a lorry with such an imposing name should be two and a half hours late struck him as being funny. It was not until later that we discovered what a gross euphemism the name really was. At twelve o'clock we were off, flying through the streets of Victoria in a cloud of dust and frightened chickens, the engine of the "Godspeed" roaring manfully to try and live up to its name.

Almost as soon as you leave Victoria you start to climb in a series of gentle loops, through apparently endless palm plantations. We had progressed some ten miles, and were just settling down. We lit cigarettes, and were arguing as to how long it would be before we reached real forest, when the engine gave a sharp hiccup, recovered itself, hiccupped again, and then slowly and apologetically faded away. We came to a gentle standstill.

"Camp Number One," said John, gazing at the endless rows of palm trees about us, serried ranks, their drooping fronds whispering in the slightest breeze.

Everyone gathered round the engine, all talking at once, and getting their fingers burnt pointing out to each other what was wrong. After about half an hour the dismembered engine was lying about all over the road, and at least four people were under the lorry, arguing loudly. I began to have a horrible feeling that this uninteresting palm grove might have to be camp number one, so I suggested to John that we should walk on up the road, and they could follow when the lorry was mended. He gazed at the bits of engine in the road, at the black legs protruding from under the bonnet, and sighed: "Yes, I suppose we can walk on. If we take it easy we have a fair chance of them catching up with us before we reach Mamfe." So we walked, but it was very dull. The palms did not foster bird life, and there were few insects in the dusty fringe of undergrowth at the roadside. Presently the lorry caught us up, everybody grinning and cheering like mad.

"I fear," said John, "that their confidence in their combined mechanical powers is misplaced."

As the "Godspeed" broke down again five miles further on, I was inclined to agree with him. The third time we broke down we had just left the last of the plantations and were entering real forest country, so it was with pleasure we dismounted and walked off down the road. The jabbering of the amateur mechanics faded away, we turned a corner, and the silence of the forest descended on us. This was our first experience of real forest, and we ambled slowly along, drinking in the sights and sounds, captivated by everything, drugged by so much beauty and colour. On one side

Sunbird

of the road was a deep ravine, choked with undergrowth, on the other side the hill-side sloped steeply upwards. On each side rose tremendous trees, straddling on their huge buttress roots, each with its cloak of parasitic plants, ferns, and moss. Through this tangle the lianas threaded their way, from base to summit, in loops and coils and intricate convolutions. On reaching the top they would drop to the forest floor as straight as a plumb line. In places there were gaps where one of the giant trees had been felled, or had fallen of its own accord, and here the secondary growth ran riot over the carcase, and everything was hung with the white and deep yellow flowers of the convolvulus, and another pink star-like flower in great profusion. In and out of these blooms flipped the Sunbirds, glinting metallically in the sun, hanging before the flowers for a brief instant on blurred and trembling wings. On the dead trees, bleached white as coral against the green, there were groups of Pygmy Kingfishers, small as a wren, brilliant in their azure blue, orange and buff plumage, with their crimson beaks and feet. Flocks of hornbills would be startled at the sight of us as they fed in the tree-tops, and would fly wildly across the road uttering loud maniacal honkings, their great untidy wings beating the air with a sound like gigantic blacksmith's bellows. We crossed numbers of wooden bridges which spanned shallow rapid streams glinting on beds of pure white sand. On the banks, where it was moist and cool, with broken sunlight dappling the grass, rested hosts of butterflies. At our approach they rose and fluttered like a small firework display in the shade, blue-gold, yellow, green and orange, shifting and changing like a kaleidoscopic picture.

Occasionally we would pass a village, a straggle of huts

along the side of the road, surrounded by small fields of
feathery cassava bushes and forlorn plantain trees with tattered leaves hanging listlessly in the sun. A band of hysterically barking curs would chase the lorry, and the pot-bellied
children would stand in the ditch, white teeth gleaming, pink
palms waving madly. At one such village we stopped and
bought a massive bunch of bananas for sixpence, and then
gorged ourselves on the delicately scented fruit until we felt
sick. Kumba was reached in the brief green twilight, as the
grey parrots were screaming overhead into the jungle to
their roosts. I made it abundantly clear to the lorry personnel
that we wanted an early start in the morning. Then we ate,
and crept tiredly under our mosquito nets.

To our surprise we were on the road by eight o'clock, and,
as if to make up for the previous day, the Godspeed went like
a bird. At midday we lunched at the roadside under the
massive trees, drinking warm beer, contesting ownership of
the sandwiches with the local ants and surveying our surroundings with the field-glasses. Bird life, as before, seemed
the most prominent: Yellow-casque Hornbills honking and
swishing in the tree-tops, kingfishers glittering on the dead
tree stumps, a beautiful rich brown and yellow Coucal with a
shrike-like beak, that peered fascinated at us while we ate.
A lovely blood-red dragon-fly zoomed down the road, flicked
sideways, and landed on the rim of my glass of beer. Six
large ants crawled slowly and methodically up my trouser
leg, and they were presently joined by a small green cater-
pillar that swung suddenly out of the sky on an almost invisible thread.

We reached Mamfe at nightfall, and soon were installed
in the great, empty, echoing rooms of the rest house, where
we watched the pale pink geckos creep out from the cracks
and scutter across the ceiling in hot pursuit of the insects our
lamp had attracted. They crept across the white ceiling almost imperceptibly, until they were near enough to a resting
moth or fly, and then they would suddenly rush in with incredible speed and snap. The next moment the insect would
have gone, and the gecko, after a short pause for gulping

and meditation, would trot off across the roof to another meal.

After getting stores and various other commodities together in Mamfe, John and I decided to split up. John wanted to go to a village called Bakebe, some twenty-five miles from Mamfe, which he thought would be a good place for birds. I, on the other hand, wished to go to Eshobi. This village is situated north of the Cross River on the edge of a section of forest that stretches unbroken and almost uninhabited hundreds of miles northwards until it reaches the desolate mountains where the gorilla has its stronghold. I felt that it would be an ideal place to set up a subsidiary camp, while John established the main base at Bakebe. While I collected mammals and reptiles I could also be obtaining birds for John, and while collecting birds in Bakebe he could also get some mammals and reptiles for me. On this plan we agreed, and I set about the task of obtaining carriers for the trek to Eshobi (for there was no road to it), and hiring a lorry to transport John to his village which was, fortunately, on a road.

The morning of our separation arrived and, with it, my ten carriers. John and I surveyed them as we ate breakfast under the trees on the rest house lawn. They were an unprepossessing lot.

"I shouldn't think", said John, eyeing them, "that you will even *reach* Eshobi with that lot. They will probably eat you before you've gone half a mile into the forest."

At this point one of the carriers yawned and displayed teeth that had been filed to points in the time-honoured cannibal way, and I was not reassured. At this moment, however, the barber arrived. It had been John who had suggested that I should get my hair

Sunbird

cut before plunging off to Eshobi, and the suggestion was sound.

As I seated myself, and the barber placed his robe reverently round me, I noticed that the carriers were dancing about, slapping themselves and cursing. I thought nothing of it until I was suddenly assailed with a series of agonizing bites on my leg, and I looked down and got my first view of a driver ant column spread out to attack. The ground was a seething black mass of ants. I roared for rescue, and two of the staff came dashing to my aid, rolled up my trousers and started to pick the ants off my legs. Just at that moment a small boy wandered on to the scene carrying two baby Drills clasped round his waist. Now I was very anxious to obtain some of these baboons, so I bargained furiously with the lad, and eventually bought them. He planted them both in my lap and departed hurriedly, for the ants were already investigating his legs. The Drills decided that this change of ownership did not appeal to them at all, and they both started to kick and scream and bite like spoilt children. The scene in the compound now beggared description: the carriers were leaping about to keep clear of the ants, our staff were trying to get the ants out of the carriers' loads, I was struggling with the drills, finding myself very much hampered by the barber's cloak, and the two members of the staff were still working on ant extermination on my upper calves. The barber had not enjoyed himself so much for years: he gazed at the lively scene, occasionally exchanging a bit of good advice or an insult with one of the carriers or the staff, and absent-mindedly chopping in the general direction of my scalp. Once, when he told a carrier which load to take, the argument waxed so fierce that I expected an ear to fall in my lap at any moment.

Eventually we sorted things out, and John accompanied us to the rusty suspension bridge which spanned the Cross River. On the other side was the forest and Eshobi. We stood there, watching the line of carriers make their way across, a hundred feet above the dark waters. As they reached the other side they were swallowed up in the multicoloured undergrowth of the forest. When the last had disappeared, and only their voices came faintly to us, I turned to John.

"Well, dear boy," I said, "I must brave the unknown. See you in about three months' time."

"Good luck," said John, and, as an afterthought, "you'll need it I expect. . . ."

I crossed the rickety, groaning planks of the bridge, the lizards darting away from me across the sun-drenched wood. At the other side I turned and waved to John, who now seemed dwarfed by the width of the river and the great trees under which he was standing. Then I turned and walked quickly down the path into the forest, anxious to catch the carriers up.

After all those months of waiting and preparation the great moment had at last arrived.

Part One

ESHOBI

CHAPTER ONE

The Forest by Day

I realized that as soon as the hunting got under way and the collection increased, most of my time would be taken up in looking after the animals, and I should not be able to wander far from camp. So I was eager to get into the forest while I had the chance, and while the camp site was still in the process of being cleared, I sent a message to the Chief of Eshobi, saying that I would like to see him. He arrived with four council members at a crucial moment when I was watching, with increasing exasperation, the efforts of five men to erect my tent, with conspicuous lack of success.

The chief was a small, bewildered-looking little man, clad in a red and gold robe, an orange stocking cap on his head, and clutching to his breast an enormous and exceedingly angry duck. The council members, an unctuous, shifty-eyed crowd, steered him through the tangle of equipment to where I stood, and then pushed him forward to say his piece. He cleared his throat, took a firmer grip on the duck, and started. It was made as difficult as possible for him by the duck, who, tried beyond endurance, flapped its wings in his face, and quacked vigorously in a hoarse and complaining way. It was so large and strong that at one point I thought it was going to take off and carry the chief with it, but he mastered it, and continued his speech a trifle breathlessly, his stocking cap askew. Having finished, he thrust the duck into my arms with relief, and I passed it on to Pious just as hurriedly.

There followed a long exchange of compliments between the chief and myself (via Pious), and an explanation as to why I had come to Eshobi. I showed him, and the council members, pictures of the various animals I wanted, and they were captivated, prodding the illustrations with their brown fingers, chortling and nodding, and ejaculating loud and appreciative "Eh . . . aehhs!" at each fresh wonder. The whole thing went down very well, and I extracted from the chief a promise that he would send to me the very best hunter in the village to act as my guide. Then I dashed him two packets of cigarettes, and he trotted off towards the village very pleased with himself. A little distance away I saw the council members close in on him and skilfully relieve him of most of the dash, ignoring his feeble protests. I turned my attention back to the tent, which had just fallen gracefully to the ground for about the sixth time.

Early the next morning two men arrived at the camp and said that they were the hunters that the chief had sent. I had them brought to the tent, and surveyed them suspiciously over my fried eggs. One was short and stocky, with a receding ape-like forehead and protruding teeth. His fat lower regions were draped in a sarong-like garment of green, covered lavishly with large orange and red flowers. The other was tall, very tall, and extremely thin. He stood there drooping artistically, drawing patterns in the dust with his long toes. His sarong was a tasteful combination of purple and white dots on a pink background.

"Good morning, Masa," said the short one, displaying his teeth in an ingratiating grin.

"Good morning, Masa," echoed the tall one, simpering at me.

"Good morning. Are *you* the hunters the chief sent?"

"Yes, sah," they chorused.

"What are your names?"

"Səh?"

"What they dey call you?" translated Pious from behind me.

"Elias, sah," said the short one in his husky voice.

"Andraia, sah," said the tall one, wriggling with embar-
rassment, and draping a long arm over his companion's
shoulders.

"Pious," said I, "ask them if they will be my hunters. I
will pay them one and six a day, and they will get dash for
every animal they catch. If it's an animal I want very much,
then the dash will be big. If it's some other kind of animal
then the dash will be smaller."

Pious listened carefully, his head on one side, then turned
to the hunters and translated rapidly into pidgin-English:

"Masa say: you go be hunter man for him, eh? Masa, he
go pay you one shilling and sixpence every day you go take
Masa and go for bush, eh? If you go catch beef kind Masa
de like *plenty*, he go dash you fine. If beef no be good Masa
go dash you small. You de hear?"

"We hear," chorused the hunters, grinning.

"You agree?"

"We agree."

"They agree, sar," said Pious to me, unnecessarily.

Then I showed them the pictures, and they responded
well to them, "Eh . . . aehhing!" as the chief had done, and
telling me where each kind of animal was to be found. With
unerring accuracy they recognized every picture I showed
them. Then I produced a picture of a camel, and asked inno-
cently if it was to be found locally. They stared at it for a
long time, chattered away to each other, and at last admitted
that they had never seen one. My spirits rose, as I had half
expected them to say that camels could be found in large
herds within half a mile of the village, such is the black man's
enthusiasm for helping the white. I told them to return the
next morning, dashed them some cigarettes, and watched
them walk off down the path with considerable misgivings,
Elias's fat-bottomed waddle in his gaudy sarong, and
Andraia mincing delicately along beside him. I had never
seen two people look less like hunters in my life, and the
more I thought about them the less faith I had in their
abilities. I was to be very pleasantly surprised, for they
turned out to be very good hunters indeed. Elias had the

courage, while Andraia had the quick-wittedness for prompt spur-of-the-moment action.

With them I was to spend many days tramping through the forest, and innumerable nights crawling through the undergrowth in the anaemic glow of the torches, searching for the lesser denizens of the bush. In a twenty-mile radius of the village they knew every path, every little stream and waterfall, almost every bush. They would melt through the thickest tangle of undergrowth with ease, and not a sound betrayed their presence, while I, hot and flat-footed, stumbled behind with a noise like a bulldozer in action. They showed me how to mark a trail, and how to follow one, and the first time I tried I was lost within ten minutes. They showed me which fruit in the bush was good to eat, and which was unpalatable, and which twigs to chew to ease your thirst without poisoning yourself.

The forest is not the hot, foetid, dangerous place some writers would have you believe; neither is it so thick and tangled as to make it impenetrable. The only place where you get such thick growth is in a deserted native farm, for here the giant trees have been felled, letting the sunlight in, and in consequence the shorter growth has a chance and sprawls and climbs its way all over the clearing, upwards towards the sun. In the deep forest the low growth has only two methods of reaching the sun: either it has to shoot upwards, smooth and branchless as a rocket-stick for hundreds of feet until it can thrust its leafy top through the canopy of trees above, or it can crawl and wind and twist its way up the giant tree trunks, and eventually arrive at the topmost branches and daylight.

As you enter the forest, your eyes used to the glare of the sun, it seems dark and shadowy, and as cool as a butter-dish. The light is filtered through a million leaves, and so has a curious green aquarium-like quality which makes everything seem unreal. The centuries of dead leaves that have fluttered to the ground have provided a rich layer of mould, soft as any carpet, and giving off a pleasant earthy smell. On every side are the huge trees, straddling on their great curling buttress roots, their great smooth trunks towering hundreds of feet above, their head foliage and branches merged indistinguishably into the endless green roof of the forest. Between these the floor of the forest is covered with the young trees, thin tender growths just shaken free of the cradle of leaf mould, long thin stalks with a handful of pale green leaves on top They stand in the everlasting shade of their parents ready for the great effort of shooting up to the life-giving sun. In between their thin trunks, rambling across the floor of the forest one can see faint paths twisting and turning. These are the roads of the bush, and are followed by all its inhabitants.

There is no life to be seen in the great forest, except by chance, unless you know exactly where to look for it. The only sounds are the incessant rasping zither of the cicadas, and a small bird who would follow you as you walked along, hiding shyly in the undergrowth and every now and then startling you with a soft, plaintive, questioning "Whooo . . . weeee?" Many times I stalked this elusive bird and heard it call from within a few feet of me, but never once did I catch a glimpse of it.

In some places where the native paths were wide the foliage overhead was broken, and through the tatter of leaves one could see patches of blue sky. The sun slanted down through these holes in the jungle covering, turning the leaves to gold, and barring the path with a hundred misty sunbeams, through which the butterflies played. Two species of these forest butterflies became favourites of mine, and on every walk I looked for them, and was rewarded by a glimpse of one or the other. The first was a small pure white insect, the delicate frosty white of snow on a window, and its flight was a joy to watch. It would rise in the air like a piece of thistledown caught in a sudden eddy of wind, and would then let itself fall earthwards, twisting and pirouetting like a miniature ballet dancer. On some paths, generally where they crossed a stream, you could encounter twenty or thirty of these delightful insects sitting motionless round the edge of a pool. Disturbed, they would rise in the air, slowly twisting and turning, gliding and falling, like a cloud of white wood ash against the green of the forest. Then they would drift back to their resting place, skimming low over the surface of the water, reflected in its darkness.

The second butterfly was a large and beautiful creature, but seen less often than the smaller white one. Its long, rather narrow wings were the most pure and vivid fire-red. Its flight was swift and erratic: suddenly in the gloom of the bushes this tantalizing flame would appear, arriving from nowhere, glimmering and glittering around, then, suddenly, like blowing out a candle, the flame was no longer there. Always the forest looked a little darker for its disappearance.

The most notable feature of the forest was the innumerable tiny streams, shallow and clear, that meandered their way in an intricate and complicated pattern across its floor. Glinting and coiling round the smooth brown boulders, sweeping in curves to form the snow-white sandbanks, busily hollowing out the earth from under the grasping tree roots, shimmering and chuckling, they went into the dark depths of the forest. They chattered and frothed importantly over diminutive waterfalls, and scooped out deep placid pools in the sandstone, where the blue and red fish, the pink crabs, and the small gaudy frogs lived. These streams, in the dry season, became the main roadways of the forest animals. Not only a roadway, but food and drink, for here congregated both the hunters and the hunted. The sandbanks would be covered with a filigree of footmarks: coral-like patterns of the bird prints, the Forest Robins, the chats, and the fat green pigeons, and occasionally the long precise toe-marks of the Pygmy Rails. On the soft earth banks you could see the great ploughed areas among the tree roots where the Red River Hogs had been rooting for tubers and giant snails, and in the soft mud you could see the long narrow slots of the boars and sows, and the tiny footprints of the piglets interlacing amongst them.

This was the forest as I was shown it by Elias and Andraia, and I found nothing frightening or dangerous about it. It was enchanting, and in the groves of towering trees with their canopy of fluttering leaves a deep silence enveloped everything, and a wonderful peacefulness prevailed.

The first day that Elias and Andraia came to take me into the forest was a memorable one, for during the time we were out I saw more animals than I ever saw again in such a short space of time . . . the gods of nature were indeed kind. My instructions to my guides were that they should lead me some five or six miles into the forest in a straight line from the village. We would then, I stated airily, walk round in a great circle with the village as the hub, so to speak. Several times during the day I regretted this plan bitterly, but I felt that my prestige was at stake on this, my first effort in the bush, and so I kept doggedly on and arrived back late that night a tattered and exhausted wreck.

We left early in the morning, and it was with relief that I heard the uproar of the camp fade away. Some twenty villagers had been engaged to build the animal house, and the noise and confusion that attended their efforts was indescribable.

We walked through the strip of farmland that surrounded the village, fields of cassava bushes and oil palms dotted with the great red earth fortresses of the Termites. I examined these massive craggy structures with interest, for I knew that in the base of each would be numerous holes in which dwelt an odd assortment of creatures besides the rightful owners of the nests. Some of them were ten feet high and twenty-five feet round the base, and the earth was baked hard as cement. Reluctantly I decided to leave investigation of these until some later date. They were near to camp and would provide some interesting trapping and digging within easy reach when the time came that I could not wander so far afield. We walked on, and presently the path crossed a small silent stream and the water was ice-cold to our feet as we waded across. We scrambled up the opposite bank, rustled and cracked our way through the low undergrowth, and burst into the forest, pausing a moment for our eyes to accustom themselves to the dimness.

We had covered about three miles, the floor of the forest

was very level and easy going when Elias, who was in front, froze in his tracks and held up his hand. We waited tensely, listening, and then Elias crept to my side and whispered:

"Na monkey, sah, 'e dere for dat big stick."

I peered up into the head foliage of "dat big stick" towering two hundred feet above us, but I could neither see nor hear a thing.

"What kind of monkey?" I asked, straining my eyes desperately.

"Na black one, sah, 'e get white mark for his face. . . .'

Putty-nose Guenon, I thought bitterly, and try as I would I could see nothing.

"Masa see 'um?"

"Not a thing."

"Masa, we go for dis side. Masa go see. . . ."

We moved off towards the place Elias indicated, drifting as silently as possible through the undergrowth. I remembered suddenly that I had my field-glasses with me, and cursing myself for a fool, I unslung them and trained them on the tree-tops. I gazed up at the shimmering ocean of leaves without success, feeling unreasonably irritated that both my hunters could obviously see and hear the monkeys, while I, even with my field-glasses, could not see a living thing. Then, suddenly, out of a mass of leaves along a great black branch, trouped a delightful procession. The first monkey was an old male, his tail crooked over his back, peering from side to side as he walked out along the branch. He was coal black, with the tips of the fur on his back tinged with green, so that he had a speckled appearance. His chest was white, and on his little black face the area on and around his nose was white also, a large heart-shaped patch as glistening white as a snowball. The hair on his head was long, and stood up straight, so that he looked not unlike a golliwog stalking disdainfully through the branches. Close on his heels came his two wives, both smaller than he, and both very timid, for they had young. The first carried a minute replica of herself slung at her breast. He was as small as a newly born kitten, and he hung under his mother's body, his long arms wrapped round her and his small hands clasping tight to the fur on her back. The other baby was older and walked cautiously behind his mother, peering fearfully down at the great drop below him, and uttering a plaintive cheeping cry. I was captivated by these babies, and as I watched them I made up my mind that I would get hold

Putty-nose Guenon

of some baby Putty-nose Guenon if I had to spend the rest of my life at it.

"Masa go shoot?" came a hoarse whisper from Elias, and lowering the glasses, I found him offering me the shotgun. For a moment I was angry that he should suggest firing at that charming family, with their golliwog heads and their white clowns' noses. But I realized it would be impossible to explain my reasons to these men: in the Cameroon forest sentimental feelings are the luxury of the well-fed. In such a place meat is hard to come by and every ounce worth its weight in gold, therefore aesthetic feelings come a very poor second to a protein-hungry body.

"No, Elias, I no go shoot," I said, and turned my glasses back to the tree-tops, but my little family had disappeared. "Elias?"

"Sah?"

"You tell men for village I go pay five shillings for one picken of that kind of monkey . . . you hear?"

"I hear, sah," said Elias, brightening visibly.

We continued our erratic way between the tree trunks, and presently came to the banks of a small stream which gurgled its way pleasantly over its shallow bed. The banks were spongy and wet, covered with a thick growth of large-leafed plants, green and succulent. We were wading through this waist-high growth, following the course of the river, when Elias suddenly leapt in the air with a yelp, and shouted, "Shoot, Masa, shoot. . . ." There was a great commotion going on ahead of me, but I could see nothing to shoot at, except Andraia, who was hopping about in the undergrowth like a lanky grasshopper, uttering cries of "Eh . . . aehh!" Judging by the noise some large animal was hidden in the greenery, but as it was thick enough to conceal anything from a leopard to a full-sized gorilla, I was not quite sure what to expect. Suddenly the animals broke cover, and I stood there gaping in amazement as a fully grown pair of Red River Hogs fled, zigzagging through the trees. They were the most vivid orange colour with long white tufts on their ears, and a flowing mane of white hair along their backs. They were quite the most startling and beautiful members of the pig family I had ever seen, and I gazed after them open-mouthed. They disappeared with extraordinary rapidity into the forest. Elias and Andraia seemed to take rather a dim view of this example of my hunting powers.

"Na bush pig dat," said Elias sadly, as we listened to the faint sound of the retreating hogs.

"Na fine chop," said Andraia wistfully, "Na fine chop for

European, too," he continued, fixing me with a reproachful
eye, in case I should think his disappointment was purely
selfish.

"This gun no got power for kill bush pig," I explained
hurriedly, "at Eshobi I get other gun much bigger."

"'E get plenty power?"

"Yes, he get plenty power, he fit kill bush pig, tiger, even
elephant," I said, boasting wildly.

"Eh . . . aehh! na true, sah?"

Red River Hog

"Na true. One day we go for bush and we go get plenty
bush pig, plenty."

"Yessir," they chorused.

We continued on our way, the hunters happy with the
thought of the roast bush pig to come, and I dwelling
pleasantly on the memory of the two beautiful beasts we had
just seen, and feeling that my prestige was still intact.

A long time after we met the Red River Hogs I was in a
considerably more exhausted condition when we had our

third and last encounter for that day. We came to an area of the forest floor which looked as though it had been ploughed up: the leaf mould had been raked and scrabbled, rocks and branches overturned, and green saplings bent and chewed. My two hunters examined the signs and then Elias crept to my side and whispered the magic word "soombo". Now soombo means a Drill, and the Drill is that prepossessing baboon one sees in the zoos with a glowing posterior and the savage frown. I always have had a soft spot in my heart for Drills, perhaps because they always display the more unmentionable parts of their bodies with such refreshing candour, to the horror of the zoo public. In any case, here, if I was to believe Elias, was a whole herd of them, and I was not going to miss the chance of seeing them in the wild state, so we crept forward with all speed in the direction of the grunts and peevish screams which we could hear echoing through the forest ahead. For an hour we followed them, scrambling and ducking, crawling on all fours, and once, rather reluctantly on my part, we traversed about a hundred yards of swamp, flat on our tummies. But try as we would, we could not get close enough for a good view, and our only reward was an occasional flash of grey fur amongst the bushes. At length we gave it up and lay exhausted on the ground, smoking much needed cigarettes and listening to the sounds of the departing drills.

We continued on our circuitous route and reached the outlying huts of the village just after dark. I was scratched and dirty and extremely tired, but I felt elated that I had done what I had set out to do. Round a bright fire outside one of the huts squatted a circle of black figures. A child ran screaming into the hut at the sudden sight of this tattered white apparition. The parents rose to greet me.

"Welcome, Masa, welcome."

"Evening, Masa . . . you done come?"

Soft voices and gleaming teeth in the firelight, and the pleasant smell of wood smoke.

"We go rest here small time, Elias," I said, and squatted down thankfully by the fire. The earth was still warm from the sun. I could feel the ache in my legs disappearing and a pleasant glow running through my body.

"Masa go for bush?" inquired the elder man of the fireside party.

"Yes, we done go for bush," said Elias importantly, and then broke into a torrent of Bayangi, gesturing into the dark forest to show the way we had gone.

There was a surprised chorus of "Eh . . . aehh's!" and more questioning. Elias turned to me, his buck teeth gleaming:

"I tell dis man, Masa, dat Masa savvay walk too much. Masa get plenty power . . ." he said, obviously thinking that I deserved flattery.

I smiled as modestly as I could.

"I tell him you get power pass black man, sah," he continued, and then jokingly, "Masa like to go for bush?"

"I like too much," I said firmly. Everyone laughed delightedly at the idea of a white man liking to go to the bush.

"Masa like to go again to bush to-night," asked Elias, his eyes bright with laughter.

"Yes, I fit go for bush to-night," I retorted, "I be hunter man, I no be woman."

A great joke this, and greeted with a roar of laughter.

"Na true, na true," said Elias, "Masa speak true."

"Masa be proper man," said Andraia, simpering at me. I passed the cigarettes round, and we squatted about the crackling fire, puffing contentedly, discussing this beef and that, until the dew started to fall heavily. Then we said good night and picked our way down the village street, redolent with the smell of palm oil, plantain and cassava—the night meal. Fires glimmered in the interiors of the huts, and at the doorways sat their owners, calling a soft greeting to us:

"Masa, you done come?"

"Welcome, Masa, welcome. . . ."

"Good night, sah!"

I felt that it was good to be alive.

CHAPTER TWO

Smoke and Small Beef

Before the news of my arrival spread through the out-lying villages, and every able-bodied man went to bush to catch animals for this madman who was buying them, and the trickle of arrivals swelled into a flood that overwhelmed me, I was able to make a number of trips into the deep forest. The object of most of these trips was not to catch animals but to find suitable spots for traps, mark hollow trees for smoking, and generally get a good idea of the surrounding forest. Unless you get to know the country you are operating in you find it almost impossible to get the animals you want, for each species has its own little section of forest, and unless you can discover where this is you stand little chance of getting specimens. Sometimes, of course, we were lucky enough to catch animals when we went on one of these expeditions: one such occasion stands out in my memory, a day when I went out accompanied only by Elias.

Andraia, I had learned, was a hypochondriac of the first order: the slightest pain or fever would drive him into the dark interior of his hut, to lie there moaning and writhing, driving his three wives into a panic lest their lord should die. This particular day he was very bad, and so Elias had promised to come by himself to accompany me to the bush. I was beginning to wish that I had not arranged to go out at all, for the afternoon heat seemed more intense than usual. There was no sound from the collection: the birds sat on their perches, their eyes half closed, the rats and porcupines sprawled asleep in their banana-leaf beds; even the energetic monkeys were drowsy and quiet. The boys' house vibrated with the combined snores of the staff, and I felt very tempted to join them in slumber. There was no breeze, the leaves hanging motionless on the trees. The heat had a dazzling, numbling quality that made you stupid and heavy. Even if you sat quite still in the shade you could still feel the sweat trickling in streams down your back and neck. Even if you sprawled in a chair you would soon find that you were sitting in a damp pool, that your shirt was black with moisture and stuck to your back and under your arms. With this heat came a heavy brooding silence: no bird songs, only the faint whisper of the cicada in the trees.

With an effort I bestirred myself to make the necessary preparations: one haversack was filled with such things as nets, cloth bags for birds or snakes, cigarettes and matches. Another smaller bag contained cartridges, a spare box of matches, the torch, and various test-tubes and jars for the smaller captures such as spiders, scorpions and their tribe. I had just finished cleaning the gun when Elias materialized outside the tent. His grinning face was beaded with sweat, in spite of the fact that he only wore a tiny scrap of dirty cloth twisted round his loins. He was carrying a short spear and the inevitable cutlass.

"Masa, I come," he greeted me. "Masa ready?"

"Yes, Elias, let's go. It's hot to-day, isn't it?"

"Sun too much," he agreed, hoisting the bags on his back.

Down the narrow red path, across the stream, ankle deep in the cool waters, pushing through the undergrowth, and then you were in the great, dim, aromatic interior of the forest, wending your way between the great trunks. After the heat of camp this was a blessed coolness that dried the sweat on your body, and the gloom allowed you to open your eyes fully, not continuously screwing them up against the sun. Elias flitted effortlessly ahead along the almost invisible path, his large feet making no sound on the leafy floor. Occasionally the forest would echo to the "chunk" of his cutlass, as he lopped off a branch that hung too low over the path for comfort. I found one difficulty in walking in the forest: there was so much to see on every side that my eyes were everywhere but on the path I was following. The gleam of a flower in the head foliage of a tree would make me peer upwards, craning my neck, or a fallen tree covered with tiny coloured toadstools, lying at the side of the path, would engage my attention, and so I would go tripping and stumbling in my efforts to see everything at once. However, this day we were going nowhere very special, so we turned aside from the path to investigate every hole, every hollow log was turned over in case it harboured scorpions or frogs, or even some larger beast in its hollow interior. So, with these deviations from the path, our progress was slow.

Some two miles from the camp we came out on to the banks of the inevitable small stream. It foamed its way through a jumble of great rocks, the tops of which were covered with thick wigs of vivid green moss and feathery ferns. In every crack that offered a foothold, a species of wild begonia grew, spreading its dark green, plate-shaped leaves against grey rock, the delicate sprays of waxy yellow flowers drooping down towards the rushing waters beneath. For an hour or so Elias and I grubbed happily around among these rocks, capturing the smaller fry: there were mottled toads, and grey tree frogs with monstrous amber eyes and long tapering fingers, and great beetles that chirruped when you picked them up. In the lush vegetation along the banks there were numbers of giant land snails, as big and as heavy as a large apple, assiduously laying their delicate pearl-like eggs in the leaf-mould. Then I discovered a beautiful green and canary-yellow frog under a small stone, and this set us both off turning over every movable stone along the bank in hopes of getting another. Elias, who was a little ahead of me, turned over a large rock and, as it rolled down the slope, he jumped back with a cry of fear.

"Masa, na snake . . . na bad beef. . . ."

I dropped everything and leapt up the slope to him. There, in the moist depression left by the boulder, lay a most remarkable snake. At first glance it appeared to have no head, being much the same circumference along its whole two feet. It was a glossy black, with a scattering of vivid red and yellow scales over different parts of its body. By staring hard I eventually located the head at one end of the body, and then I noticed that the head was only a matter of inches from a round hole that went deep into the earth. I was determined not to lose this spectacular addition to the collection so, with the aid of a stick, I gently rolled a small stone inch by inch nearer until it covered the mouth of the hole. Elias stood discreetly in the background and moaned:

"Masa, 'e go bite you. Careful, masa, na bad beef dat. . . ."

The snake made no move beyond flicking its tongue in and out rather rapidly. Having cut off its retreat I felt better.

"Masa, dat kind of beef get poison too much. . . ."

"Elias, shut up and go and bring me a big bag and another stick."

"Yessir," said Elias dismally, and wandered off.

The snake lay absolutely still watching me in a circumspect manner, and I kept my small twig ready in case it should try to make a sudden dash for it. I was fairly sure that it was harmless, but with such garish coloration I was taking no chances. Elias returned panting with the cloth bag and a long stick. Gently I manœuvred the mouth of my bag until it was only a few inches away from the snake's head, then I tapped it gently on the tail with my stick. I was prepared for a certain amount of reluctance on the snake's part to enter the bag, but I was not prepared for what happened. Feeling the stick on its tail the snake coiled itself rapidly into a knot, and then suddenly leapt forwards like a released spring, straight into the bag. There it lay as still as before, while we hastily tied the neck of the bag up. I had never met such an accommodating reptile.

"Eh . . . aehh!" said Elias, in amazement, "dis snake no get fear. I tink dis snake like Masa," and he chuckled away to himself for a long time as we continued turning over boulders.

This snake turned out to be a Calabar Ground Python, a

small relative of the great constricting snakes. Both the head and the tail taper off in the same way, and as the whole body is covered with small, round, even scales, it is difficult to see where the snake begins and ends, so to speak. The small eyes are exactly the same size, shape and colour as the scales surrounding them, so it is difficult to pick them out. The pattern of coloured scales on the black background is not really a pattern: the coloured scales are simply scattered about haphazardly, so the markings give you no clue as to which end of the snake you are looking at. It is a completely harmless creature, spending most of its time burrowing in moist earth, searching for the small prey its weak jaws can accommodate. When held in the hand it would coil itself up, and then suddenly spring forward in the way I have described, but it would never attempt to bite, or even coil round one's restraining hand and try to crush it, as even a baby of the larger species will try to do.

This Ground Python was our first real capture of the day, and we continued on our way feeling very elated. But although we turned over every boulder we could move, we did not find another. Presently we packed up the tins and bags and moved on, leaving the river bank in a state of upheaval that could only have been equalled by a troop of drill or forest hogs. Our final objective was a small grass field some five miles from the village; Elias had discovered this place some days ago and had told me that he thought it a likely place for beef . . . what kind of beef he did not specify. It transpired that he had not marked the route as well as usual, and so we at length came to a halt and Elias reluctantly admitted that he did not know exactly where we were, either in relation to the village, or the grass field. I sat down firmly on a large log and refused to move until he could assure me that he knew which way we were going.

"I will stay here, you go and look the path. When you find 'um you come back here for me, you hear?"

"Yessir," said Elias cheerfully, and disappeared through the trees. For a few minutes I could hear the ring of his cutless marking the trail, and then this grew fainter and eventu-

46

ally faded away. I lit a cigarette and surveyed my domain. Suddenly, from the very log on which I was sitting, a cicada lifted up its voice. I sat very still and scanned the bark carefully. These cicadas were the bane of my existence: they were everywhere in the forest, and they sang their loud vibrating songs both day and night, yet try as I would, I had never yet succeeded in seeing one. Now, apparently, there was one zithering away within a foot of me, if I could spot him. I examined the trunk carefully, the green spongy moss, the minute clusters of crimson and yellow toadstools huddled in the cracks, the dead lianas still clutching their host's body in a grip that had bitten into the bark. A trail of ants wended their way through this miniature scenery, and at the mouth of a small hole a black spider crouched immobile. But no sign of a cicada. Then, as I moved my head slightly, I caught a sudden gleam from the moss, as from glass. Looking closely I saw the insect: its body was about two inches long, and patterned in an intricate and beautiful filigree of silver and leaf-green, merging perfectly with the green moss and the grey bark of the trunk. Its great wings, which gleamed like glass when the sun caught them, were the things that had attracted my attention. Gently I brought my cupped hand down over it, and then suddenly I grabbed. The cicada, finding itself detected and captured, started to flutter its wings wildly, and they rustled like paper against my fingers. Then, in desperation, it uttered its prolonged shrill cry. I held it gently in my hand and examined it: the silver and green body was nut hard, and the eyes large and protuberant. The wings were like sheets of mica, and when held up to the light revealed a tracery of veins as complicated and beautiful as a cathedral window. Between its legs, set in a groove, was its long thin proboscis. With this fragile instrument it pierces the bark of the trees and gorges on the sap beneath. Having examined it I set it upright on the palm of my hand, where it sat for a minute, nervously vibrating its lovely wings before zooming off into the trees.

I was wondering if I could keep these insects alive in a netting cage on a diet of honey and water, and so get them back to England, when Elias returned. He had discovered the path, he said, and now knew where he was.

We rejoined the path and resumed our way towards the grass field. These grass fields are formed in certain areas of the forest where the soil is too shallow to support the probing roots of the huge trees. A low clinging growth covers this space, a growth that can exist with its wiry roots clinging to the few inches of soil covering the great carapace of rock that forms the foundation to the forest. So the tough grasses come into their own, spreading across the clearing; in the cracks in the rocks, where the rains have washed the soil into deeper pockets, tiny stunted trees get a foothold and flourish. But these small fields are ringed about by the tall forest: should the depth of soil increase the great trees scatter their seed and slowly usurp this territory from the grip of this lowly vegetation.

Presently the trees grew thinner, the light grew stronger, and we came to a thick tangle of low growth that bordered the clearing. We pushed our way through this flower-hung, thorny curtain, and found ourselves knee-deep in long grass, the clearing sloping away from us like a great meadow, golden-green in the sun, quiet and lonely, its borders fringed with the towering ramparts of the forest.

We lay down in the warm crisp grass and lit cigarettes. We lay there, basking in the sun, and gradually the sounds of the life in the clearing came floating to us: the ringing cries of the big pink-winged locusts; a tree frog piping shrilly from the banks of the tiny trickle of water that curled through the grass; the soft and husky coo of a small dove, perched in the bushes above us. Then, from the far side of the clearing, a series of loud care-free cries rang out, echoing among the trees: "Carroo . . . carroo . . . coo . . . coo . . . coo. . . ."

Again and again, echoing loud across the shimmering grass. I trained my field-glasses on to the trees at the far side of the clearing and searched the branches carefully. Then I saw them, three large glittering green birds, with long heavy tails and curved crests. They took flight, straight as arrows, across the clearing, and landed in the trees the opposite side, and as they landed they shouted their challenging cry again. As they called, as though in an excess of high spirits, they leapt from branch to branch in great rabbit-like leaps, and raced along the branches like racehorses, as easily as though the branches had been roads. They were a flock of Giant Plantain-eaters, perhaps the most beautiful of the forest birds. I had often heard their wild cries in the forest, but this was my first sight of them. Their acrobatic powers amazed me, as they leapt and bounded, and ran amongst the branches, pausing now and then to pluck a fruit and swallow it, and then shout to the forest. As they flew from tree to tree in the sun, trailing their tails behind them like giant magpies, they shimmered green and gold, a breathtakingly beautiful colour.

"Elias, you see those birds?"

"Yessir."

"I go give ten shillings for one of those alive."

"Na true, sah?"

"Na true. So you go try, eh?"

"Yessir . . . ten shillings . . . eh . . . aehh!" said Elias, as he lay back in the grass to enjoy the last puffs of his cigarette.

I sat back and watched the gorgeous shining birds leap and twist their way into the maze of trees, shouting joyfully to each other, and then silence descended on the grass field again.

Presently we set to work. The long nets with the small mesh were unpacked, and these we arranged in a half-circle, the lower edge buried in the soil. They were hung rather loosely, so that any animal running into them would become entangled in the folds. Then, from point to point of the nets, we cleared the undergrowth away in a strip some two feet wide, and, cutting grass, we laid this along the line, and covered it lightly with damp leaf mould. Now we had a complete circle, half formed by the nets, the other half by this line of dry grass. Then we proceeded to drench the grass with kerosene and set light to it. The damp leaf-mould prevented the tinder-like grass from burning quickly, so it smouldered gently, letting a thin curtain of pungent smoke drift towards the nets. We waited expectantly, but nothing happened. Only a host of big locust fled from the smoke, hopping and whirring agitatedly. We put out the fire, moved the nets to a fresh area, and repeated the performance with the same results. Our eyes smarted with the smoke, and we were scorched by the fire and the sun. Six times we moved the nets, laboriously laid the fires, and still caught nothing for our pains.

I was beginning to doubt Elias's judgment of this grass field as a good place for beef, when on the seventh pitch we struck lucky. Scarcely had we set fire to the grass when I saw a portion of the net start to quiver and jerk. I rushed through

Pouched Rat with Domestic Mouse

the smoke and found a large grey animal with a long scaly tail struggling in the folds of the net. I caught him swiftly by the tail and swung him aloft: it was a Pouched Rat, as big as a kitten, his grey fur full of the large cockroach-like parasites that inhabit these beasts.

"Elias, I get ground beef," I shouted. But he was too busy at another part of the net to heed me, so with some difficulty I succeeded in getting the rat into a thick canvas bag without getting myself bitten. I approached the other end of the net through the smoke, and found Elias darting about on all fours grunting and mumbling angrily:

"Ah, you blurry ting you . . . ah, you bad beef. . . ."

"What is it, Elias?"

"Na bush rat, sah," he said excitedly, "'e de run too fast, and 'e de bite too much . . . careful, sah, 'e go chop you. . . ."

In and out of the tussocks of grass ran a host of rats, dancing and jumping with speed and agility, retreating before the smoke, yet avoiding the mesh of the net with extraordinary efficiency. They were fat and sleek, with olive green bodies, and their noses and behinds were a bright rusty red. They ran through our legs, leapt in and out of the grass, their little pink paws working overtime, and their long white whiskers twitching nervously. They were quite fearless, and they bit like demons. As Elias knelt down to try and catch one in the grass, another ran up his leg, burrowed rapidly under his loin-cloth, and bit him in the groin. It dropped to the ground and disappeared into the grass.

"Arrrrr!" roared Elias. "'E done chop me, sah . . . eh . . . aehh! na bad beef dis ting. . . ."

But one had just fastened its teeth into my thumb, so I was too occupied to take much interest in Elias's honourable wounds. In the end we captured ten of these rats, and emerged from the smoke looking as though we had been having a rough and tumble with a leopard. I had five painful bites on my hands and my face was scratched where I had fallen into a large and evil bush. Elias's legs were streaming with blood and he had two bites on his hands and one on his knee. It is astonishing how one bleeds in the tropics: the slightest scratch and the blood flows out freely as though you had severed an artery. Our sweat was trickling into these open bites and scratches and making them smart furiously. Our hair was full of mud and ashes. I decided that the rats had made us pay dearly for their capture.

We decided to smoke one more patch of grass before starting for home. The tedious business of setting up the nets and laying the fires we now performed cheerfully, for the captures had elated us, as captures of any sort always did. There is nothing so depressing as repeating a thing over and over again with no results. We stood back expectantly and watched the smoke curl sluggishly into the golden grass.

The first thing to break cover and make for the nets, under the impression that the grass field was on fire, were two beautiful, richly coloured skinks. One I captured with the butterfly net, but the other rushed at Elias, who made a half-hearted swipe at it with a stick, and then stood watching the reptile scuttle off into the bushes.

"Elias, you haven't lost it? . . ."

"'E go for bush, sah," said Elias dismally.

"Why you no catch um . . . you no get hand?" I inquired angrily, brandishing my skink under his nose by way of illustration. He backed away hurriedly.

"Masa, na bad beef dat. If 'e go bite you, you go die."

"Nonsense," I retorted, and I pushed my little finger between the lizard's half-open jaws and let him bite. It was no more than a slight pinch.

"You see? He no be bad beef. He no fit bite proper, no get power."

Yellow-spotted Rat

"Masa, 'e get poison," said Elias, watching fascinated while the skink chewed on my finger. "Na bad beef, sah, for true."

"Well, if he bite me I go die, no be so?"

"No, sah," said Elias, with one of those wonderful twists of African logic which are impossible to argue against, "you be white man. If dat beef go chop black man he go die one time. White man different."

I placed my skink in a cloth bag and we turned our attention back to the nets, in which were struggling three lovely rats, and a black, evil-looking shrew. The rats were a pale fawn colour, and covered with longitudinal lines of round, intense, cream-coloured spots. When we picked them up by their tails they hung relaxed and quiet, and we even handled them without receiving a bite. Later I found that these rats, although extremely timid, were the most easily tamed of the forest rats; after two days of captivity they would climb on to the palm of one's hand to be fed.

The shrew, on the other hand, had a temper as black as his fur. Although he was a bare three inches long he struggled fiercely in the net, and as we tried to disentangle him he attacked us, his mouth open, and his long nose wiffling with rage. Once free of the net he sat up on his hind legs, bunched his tiny paws into fists, and shrieked defiance at us, daring us to touch him. With great difficulty we coaxed him into a box, where he sat, up to his waist in the dry grass with which I had filled it, and muttered wickedly to himself. I did not intend to keep him, for it was doubtful if such a tiny mite could survive the long and arduous voyage to England, but I wanted to keep him for a few days and study him at close range. To the Africans the fact that I sometimes went to all the trouble of capturing an animal, only to keep it for a few days and then release it again, unharmed and uneaten, was sure proof that I was somewhat weak-minded.

The sun was slanting across the grass field as we packed up and left, turning the edge of the forest into a wall of glittering golden-green leaves. Darkness overtook us rapidly in the forest, and soon it was pitch dark beneath the trees. I stumbled along, tripping over roots and banging my head on branches to the accompaniment of innumerable "Sorry, sah's" from Elias. When we reached the fields around the village we found it was that moment of twilight before night enveloped the world: a pair of parrots flew swiftly into the forest at a great height above us, their screams and whistles echoing down to us. The scattered clouds were flushed gold and pink and green. The lights of the camp gleamed a welcome to us, and the smell of groundnut chop was wafted to my nostrils. I realized, rather ruefully, that before I could have a bath and some food, all the captures would have to be housed and fed.

53

CHAPTER THREE

Bigger Beef

The bigger beef were almost as numerous as the small
ones: they consisted of anything from the size of a
domestic cat to that of an elephant. The bigger beef
were, as a rule, much more easily captured, simply because
they were more easily seen. After all, a creature the size of
a mouse or squirrel does not need much undergrowth to
conceal itself in, whereas something the size of a duiker
does. Also the smaller beasts had an irritating habit of
squeezing through the mesh of your nets, whereas once the
bigger beef ran into a net you were fairly certain that it was
yours.

One morning Elias and Andraia arrived at what seemed
to me a most ungodly hour. Lying in the gloom of the tent I
could hear them outside arguing in fierce whispers with
Pious as to whether or not I was to be disturbed. Pious was
a martinet on this point; it took a long time for me to teach
him that newly arrived animals could not wait for attention.
If someone arrived with a specimen while I was shaving, or
eating, or cleaning the gun, Pious would majestically order
him to wait. The poor specimen, having already endured a
none too gentle capture, probably a day without food and
water, and a long walk in the sun in an uncomfortable bag
or sack, would probably expire with this additional wait.
This applied particularly to birds. At first I could not get the
bird trappers to understand that if they caught a bird last
thing at night, and did not bring it to me until the following

54

morning, its chances of living were so slight they were not worth considering. Always, when this was explained, I would get the same answer: "Masa, dis na strong bird. Dis bird no fit die, Masa, for true."

In view of this attitude among the hunters I had to explain to Pious that an animal could not wait, and whatever time a specimen arrived, in the middle of lunch or the middle of the night, it was to be brought straight to me. After a great deal of shouting I thought that I had driven the point home, yet here he was keeping Elias and Andraia away from me: I presumed, from the argument going on outside the tent, that he had forgotten his instructions. It seemed evident that Elias and Andraia had been out into the forest rather early, and that they had got something and were anxious that I should purchase it before it died on their hands, while Pious was determined that I should not be disturbed before the lawful hour of six-thirty. I was annoyed.

"Pious!" I roared.

"Sah?"

After a pause he came into the tent bearing a steaming cup of tea in one hand. This placated me somewhat.

"Good morning, sah."

"Good morning," I answered, clutching the cup. "What's all that row outside? Someone brought beef?"

"No, sah, Elias and Andraia come to take you for bush."

"Good Lord, at this hour. Why so early?"

"They say", said Pious, in a disbelieving tone of voice, "they find a hole for ground, very far."

"A hole for ground . . . you mean a cave?"

"Yes, sah."

This was good news, for I had told the hunters to find some caves for us to investigate, but hitherto they had met with no success. I crawled out of bed and went forth resplendent in my blue and red dressing-gown.

"Good morning, Elias . . . Andraia."

"Good morning, sah," as usual in a chorus, like Tweedledum and Tweedledee.

"What's all this about a hole?" I asked, sipping my tea

with a lordly air. They tore their fascinated eyes away from my dressing-gown with an effort.

"Yesterday I done go for bush, Masa," said Elias, "I done find hole for ground like Masa de want. Dare be some kind of beef dere for inside, I hear um."

"You see dis beef?"

"No, sah, I no see um," said Elias, shuffling his feet. Being by himself, I realized, he would not have ventured into the cave, for the noise may have been produced by a malignant *ju-ju* of some description.

"All right, what we go do, eh?"

"Masa, we go get four men and we go for bush. We go take catch-net and we catch dis beef. . . ."

"All right, go for village and find some good hunter men. Then you go come back in one hour, you hear?"

"We hear, sah," and they went off to the village.

"Pious, I want breakfast at once."

"Yes, sah," said Pious mournfully. He had been afraid of this. He whisked off to the kitchen and raised hell with the cook to relieve his feelings. "You no hear Masa say he want breakfast *now* . . . you go sit there like bushman, eh? Gimme plate, gimme cup, quick, quick."

Within an hour we were deep in the forest, climbing up a great hill-side between the twisting roots of the trees. Besides Elias and Andraia there were three other men: a shifty, fox-faced individual known as Carpenter, by virtue of his trade; a boisterous likeable youth called Nick; and a gaunt, taciturn person called Thomas. Daniel the animal boy followed behind carrying the food supply for the party. We were all in high spirits, the hunters conversing loudly, laughing and ejaculating "eh . . . aehh!" at intervals, the ringing "chunk" of their cutlasses biting into the wood as they marked the trail. We climbed steadily for about half a mile, and then the forest floor levelled out, and walking became easier. In certain places we came across a tree, about six inches in circumference, growing straight and branchless as a wand up into the maze of foliage above. The trunk of this tree was covered with numbers of tiny waxy blossoms, a deep and beautiful pink, growing on a minute stem about a quarter of an inch long. The flowers were about the size of one's little finger-nail, and grew so close together that they completely hid great sections of the bark. In the strange, underwater light of the forest these trees glowed against the dark background like great spiky sticks of pink coral. In one place we passed six of these trees growing out of a hillock of big boulders, which were covered with green velvet-like moss, and the flowers of the yellow begonias. One could walk for hours in the forest, and just as one's eyes were getting tired of the never-ending sameness of the smooth, branchless trunks, and the thin wispy undergrowth, you would suddenly come upon a scene like this, fantastic in colour and grouping, and your interest would be revived by its beauty.

At one point in our journey I discovered alongside the path we were following the immense rotting carcase of a tree, a hundred and fifty feet of it, stretching its great length across the floor of the forest. Although it had fallen some considerable time ago, you could still see how it had splintered and bent the smaller growth around it, and the great weight of the head foliage had ripped its way earthwards, creating a small clearing where it had fallen and leaving a gap in the forest roof so that you could see an area of blue sky above. The roots had been torn from the earth, twisted and black they looked like a giant hand. In the palm of this hand was the dark entrance to the hollow interior of the trunk. I called Elias's attention to it, and he considered it gravely.

"You think there be beef for inside?"

"Sometime there go be beef for inside," he admitted cautiously.

"All right, we go look. . . ."

Andraia, the Carpenter, and the mournful Thomas went to the top end of the trunk while Nick, Elias, and myself investigated the hole in the base. On close inspection this entrance hole proved to be some eight feet in diameter, and one could stand up in it with comfort. Elias and Nick crawled a few feet into the hollow interior, and sniffed like terriers. All I could smell was the rotting wood and damp earth.

"Ah," said Elias, sniffing furiously. "Na catar beef, eh, Nick?"

"I tink so," agreed Nick, also sniffing.

I sniffed again, but could still smell nothing.

"What", I inquired of Elias, "is a catar beef?"

"Na big beef, sah. 'E get skin for 'e back like snake. He go so . . ." and he hunched himself into a ball to illustrate the habits of the animal.

"Well, how are we going to get it out?" I asked.

Elias emerged from the trunk and carried on a rapid conversation in Banyangi with the Carpenter at the other end of the tree. Then he turned to me: "Masa get flashlamp?"

"Yes. . . . Daniel, bring dat flashlamp from bag. . . ."

With the torch in his mouth Elias once more got down on all fours and disappeared into the interior of the tree with much grunting and echoing gasps of "Eh . . . aehh!" I did not feel it was an opportune moment to remind him that some species of snake delight in living in such hollow places. I wondered what he would do if he came upon a snake in that tunnel-like trunk, with no room to turn.

Suddenly, about twenty feet down the trunk, we heard great knockings and muffled shouts.

"Na whatee . . . na whatee?" yelled Nick excitedly. A flood of Banyangi echoed along the hollow trunk to us.

"What's he say?" I begged Nick, my visions of a deadly snake becoming more convincing.

"Elias say he see beef, sah. He say 'e dere for inside. He say make Carpenter put small fire and smoke go make beef run, den Elias he catch um."

"Well, go and tell the Carpenter."

"Yessir. You get matches, sah?"

I handed over my matches, and Nick bounded off to the other end of the tree. I crawled into the interior and dimly I could see the glow of the torch that indicated Elias's position, far down the trunk.

"Elias, are you all right?"

"Sah?"

"Are you all right?"

"Yessah. I see um, sah," he called excitedly.

"What kind of beef?"

"Na catar beef, sah, and 'e get picken for 'e back."

"Can I come and see?" I pleaded.

"No, sah, no get chance here. Dis place too tight, sah," he called, and then he started to cough. A great cloud of pungent smoke swept down the trunk, obliterating the torch light, filling my lungs and making my eyes water. Elias was making the interior vibrate with his coughing. I crawled out hurriedly, with streaming eyes.

"Andraia," I yelled, "you make too much smoke . . . you go kill Elias and the beef together . . . put the fire out, make it small, you hear?"

"Yes, sah, I hear," came faintly from the other end of the tree.

Once more I crawled into the smoke-filled interior.

"You all right, Elias?"

"I get um, sah, I get um," screamed Elias delightedly, between coughs.

"Bring um," I called, crawling frantically round on all fours in an endeavour to see through the smoke, "bring um quick. . . ." It seemed hours before the horny soles of his feet appeared in the entrance, and he emerged choking and coughing and stark naked, the capture wrapped in his loin-cloth. He grinned at me excitedly.

"I put um for my cloth, sah," he said. "I fear sometime de picken go fall."

"Dis beef run fast?" I inquired, carrying the mysterious heavy bundle out to a clear spot before unwrapping it.

"No, sah."

"He bite?"

"No, sah."

Fortified with this knowledge I placed the bundle on the ground and unwrapped it. There appeared before my eyes the most extraordinary beast. A first glance at the contents of the loin-cloth showed me what seemed to be a gigantic brown fir cone, with a smaller pink-grey coloured cone adhering to it. Then I realized that it was a female Pangolin, or Scaly Anteater, rolled tight into a ball, with her tiny pale youngster clinging to her back.

"Catar beef, sah," said Elias proudly.

Pangolin

"Na fine beef dis," I said.

With difficulty I removed the baby from its mother's back to have a look at it. It was, unlike its mother, quite fearless, and sat on the palm of my hand peering at me my-opically out of its small rheumy eyes, exactly like two dull and protuberant boot buttons. It was about ten inches long from the tip of its long snout to the tip of its scaly tail, and its back, head, legs and tail were covered with tiny, over-lapping, leaf-shaped scales which, as it was so young, were this pale pinkish-grey and still soft. His tummy, chin, insides of his legs, and his sorrowful face were covered with whitish, rather coarse fur, and the underside of his tail was quite bare. His face was long, and his wet and sticky nose he kept trying to push between my fingers. The fat little hind paws were neatly clawed, but the front feet possessed one great curved claw, bordered on each side by a smaller claw. With these front claws the baby clung to my hand with incredible strength, and tried to coil his tail round my wrist for extra safety, but this part of his anatomy had not yet got the strength of the adult, so that every time he coiled it round, it slipped off. His mother was the same to look at, except that her scales were hard and chestnut brown in colour, and the edges were worn and broken, not finished off neatly in three little spikes as the baby's were. As far as I could judge, for she resisted unrolling with a becoming modesty, she must have measured about three feet in length. Curled up she was the size of a football.

The hunters, of course, were wildly enthusiastic over this capture: but I was remembering all that I had read about pangolins, and was inclined to take a gloomy view. Pangolins are anteaters: they possess no teeth, but a very long, snake-like tongue and a copious supply of very sticky saliva. With their great front claws they rip open the ants' nests, and then their long tongues flick in and out, and on each return journey there is a layer of ants adhering to it. As is the case with all animals that have such a restricted diet, they do not take kindly to a substitute food in captivity, and have so earned the reputation of being extremely difficult to keep alive. However, they were my first pangolins, and I was determined that I would not give in without a struggle. I replaced the baby on its mother's back, and he clung on with his great front claws stuck in a crack between two scales, and the tip of his tail hooked into another. Then, having anchored himself, he put his long nose between his front paws and went to sleep. We placed them both in a canvas bag and then continued on our way.

An hour's walk brought us to the cave that Elias had been so anxious to get me to: a steep hill-side covered with enormous rocks tumbled about its lower slopes, some of them half buried in the earth, and some almost hidden under a dense growth of ferns, begonias, and thick moss. Under one of these rocks was an opening some three feet long and eighteen inches high. Elias pointed at it proudly.

"Na hole, sah," he explained.

"Is *this* the cave?" I inquired, inspecting the tiny opening suspiciously.

"Yes, sah. 'E get small door, but 'e get plenty room for inside. . . . Masa go look with flashlight?"

"All right," I said resignedly.

They cleared away the undergrowth from the mouth of the cave, and then, lying on my stomach, I insinuated my head and shoulders into the opening. Sure enough, the interior of the cave was the size of a small room, and at the far end the floor seemed to slope steeply down into the depths of the hill-side. The air smelt fresh and cold. The floor of the cave was of solid rock, sprinkled with pure white sand. I wriggled out again.

"Someone", I said firmly, "will have to go inside and hold the torch, then we can follow." I surveyed the hunters, none of whom showed any eagerness to volunteer for this duty. I picked out Daniel as being the smallest.

"You, Daniel, take the flashlight and go for inside. Andraia and I go follow. . . ."

Both Daniel and Andraia seemed reluctant.

"Masa," whined Daniel, "sometime dere go be beef for inside. . . ."

"Well?"

"Sometime 'e go catch me. . . ."

"You no be hunter?" I inquired, frowning severely. "If you be hunter how beef go catch you? *You* go catch *beef*, no be so?"

"I de fear," said Daniel simply.

"Elias," I said, "go listen if you can hear beef for inside."

Each, in turn, pushed his woolly head into the hole, and each said that they could not hear anything.

"You see?" I said to Daniel. "Now you go for inside. No fear, we no go leave you. Andraia and I go follow you one time."

With the air of a martyr approaching the stake, Daniel lowered himself to the ground and crawled into the hole.

"Now, Andraia, in you go. . . ."

Andraia's six and half feet took some time to get inside, and we could hear him abusing Daniel roundly, first for sitting right in the entrance (or, from Daniel's point of view, the exit), and secondly for shining the torch in his eyes. Eventually he disappeared from view, and I prepared to follow him. Just as my head and shoulders were inside a series of loud shrieks burst forth from the cave, I was hit sharply on the head with the handle of the butterfly net, and the torch was flashed in my eyes so that I could not see what was happening.

"Masa, Masa," yelled Daniel, hitting me again with the butterfly net, "na big boa . . . na big snake. . . . Go back, sah, go back. . . ."

"Shut up," I roared, "and stop hitting me with that bloody net."

Daniel subsided into a trembling heap, and I crawled in and crouched beside him, taking charge of the torch. I flashed it around and located Andraia's lanky body sitting next to me.

"Andraia, which side dis boa?"

"I no see um, sah," he answered. "Daniel 'e say 'e see um for dere . . ." and he gestured with a long arm into the deep passage in front of us.

"You *see* um?" I asked Daniel, whose teeth were chattering.

"Yessah, I see um for true, sah, 'e dere dere for inside. 'E get mark mark for his skin, sah. . . ."

"All right. Be quiet and listen."

We crouched in silence, only broken by the chattering of

Daniel's teeth. Suddenly I became aware of another sound in the cave, and by the way Andraia cocked his head on one side I could see that he also heard it. It was a faint hissing, purring noise, welling up out of the darkness ahead of us. Daniel started to moan, and I rapped him sharply on the shins with my torch.

"You hear it, Andraia . . . na whatee?" I whispered.

"I no savvy, sah," said Andraia, in a puzzled voice.

The noise had a rather ominous and malignant quality, coming from the darkness. The atmosphere of the cave was icy, and we were all shivering. I felt that something must be done, or else in another minute Daniel would attribute the noise to some form of *ju-ju*, and then I should be trampled to death in the rush to get out of the tiny opening. Taking the torch I told my shivering hunters to stay where they were and started to crawl forward to the place where the cave sloped down into the bowels of the earth. I did not relish this exploration very much, for I felt that this was not the place to have words with a python of unknown size, particularly as one hand was fully occupied holding on to my only source of illumination. On reaching the edge I leant forward and shone the torch, peering down into the large cave below me. From its interior the noise was coming, and as I flooded it with light it seemed to me that the whole roof of the lower cave left its moorings and swept up towards me in a great gust of wind and ghostly twittering. For one heart-stopping moment, as this great black mass swept towards me, I wondered if my treatment of *ju-ju* had not been a trifle off hand. Then I realized that this great cloud was composed of hundreds of tiny bats. The air was thick with them, like a swarm of bees, and the roof of the lower chamber was still covered with hundreds more, like a furry, moving rug over the rock face. Twittering they wheeled round me, flicking in and out of the torch beam, creating a tremendous fluttering wind with their beating wings. I probed the cave below with the torch beam, but I could see no sign of Daniel's "boa".

"Andraia," I called, "no be boa, na bat. . . ."

Thus encouraged, Andraia and Daniel scuttled across and joined me.

They peered down into the bat-filled cave.

"Eh . . . aehh !" said Andraia.

Daniel said nothing, but his teeth stopped chattering.

"Now", I said to him sarcastically, "which side dat big boa, eh?"

He started to giggle, and Andraia joined in.

"All right. Now let's have no more foolishness, you hear? Go for outside and ask Elias for the rope and the catch-net . . . quickly."

Daniel scrambled off to the entrance.

"Masa want dis kind of beef?" inquired Andraia, while we were waiting for Daniel's return.

"No, I no want dis small-small bat; I want the big kind. Some time we go find um for inside, you think?"

"By God Power, we go find um," said Andraia piously, peering into the depths.

To get to the lower cave we would have to lower ourselves down the steep fifteen-feet slope of rock, on the edge of which we were now squatting. Ropes were the only answer, and I looked about for something to tie the end to. There was nothing. In the end, when Daniel had returned with the ropes and net, we had to send him back with one end of the rope and instructions that it was to be tied to a tree outside. This done, we covered the tunnel that joined the two caves with our net, left Daniel sitting there to disentangle any bats that flew into it, and Andraia and I descended into the depths. The slope, at first sight, appeared to be smooth, but on close contact with it we discovered that the surface was covered with fine longitudinal furrows, like a ploughed field, and the ridges between the furrows had an edge like a razor. At length, torn and bloody, we reached the sandy cave floor. Here the bats were so thick that the air vibrated with their cries and the flutterings of their wings. With Andraia holding the torch, I leapt about with the long-handled net, and after much exertion I succeeded in catching four of these small bats. I wanted them merely as museum specimens, for small insect-eating bats such as these are difficult to keep alive, and would not survive the long journey home. They had a wing-span of about eight inches, and their fat, furry bodies were about the size of a walnut. But it was their heads that astonished me, as I examined them by the light of the torch. Their great, petal-shaped ears stood up from their heads, transparent in the torchlight. On their noses the flesh was bare, and fluted and curled and scalloped into an incredible bas-relief design, like a misshapen Tudor rose in miniature. These gargoyles' tiny eyes glittered, and their teeth shone white in their open mouths.

After this we searched to see if any of the larger fruit-eating bats shared the caves with these little monsters, but we searched in vain. We sent Daniel up to the surface with the nets, and then I followed. As I crawled, blinking, out into the sunlight, the Carpenter rushed forward to help me to my feet.

"Welcome, sah," he said, as though I had been on a long journey.

"You think *ju-ju* done get me, Carpenter?"

"No, sah, but sometimes you go get bad beef for dis kind of place."

"And *ju-ju*?"

"Ehh . . . sometime you get *ju-ju* also," he admitted.

Andraia now emerged, scratched and earthy, and we sat in the sun to get the chill of the caves out of our bones.

"Which side Elias?" I asked, having just noticed his absence.

"He go come small time, sah," said the Carpenter, "he done go for bush look some other hole."

"Is there another hole?" I asked eagerly.

The Carpenter shrugged.

"Sometime Elias go find one," he answered, not very hopefully.

But the Carpenter was wrong. When Elias returned he said that he had found another cave, about half a mile away, which was bigger than the one we had just investigated and, moreover, was full of large bats. We followed Elias there with all speed.

Sure enough, this second cave was bigger than the first: it was a great hollow carved into a cliff face on the hill-side, its mouth almost hidden by undergrowth. Inside it proved to be some seventy yards long, and the roof was at least thirty feet high. This was covered with a thick palpitating layer of squeaking fruit bats. It was a most encouraging sight, and I congratulated Elias on this find. However, soon difficulties became apparent: the roof of the cave was too high to reach even with the long-handled nets we had, and the mouth of the cave was so large that we could only cover part of it with our big net. After considerable thought I formed a plan. Two of the hunters were sent into the surrounding forest to cut us each a sapling about twenty feet long; these were then carefully trimmed, leaving only a bunch of twigs and leaves at one end. Having covered as much of the entrance as we could with our nets, I then armed each man with a soft cloth bag to put his catch in. Then I stepped back, and, aiming the shotgun at the floor in the interior of the cave I let fly with both barrels. Then the sudden roar of the gun, and the subsequent echoes, were overwhelmed and lost in the pandemonium that broke loose in the cave. The entire colony of bats, which must have numbered about five hundred, took flight, and as they wheeled and flapped their way, panic-stricken, round the cave, they shrieked and chattered. The noise of their wings beating the air was like the sound of heavy surf on a rocky coast. Pausing long enough to make sure that the roof of the cave was not in imminent danger of collapse from the shock of the explosion, we rushed inside. The air was thick with fruit bats, flying low over our heads, swooping to within a foot of our faces before twisting to one side, leaving our hair ruffled with the wind from their wings. We set to work, and dashed round the cave, whirling our sticks above our heads as we ran. It was useless to try and aim at a bat, for they simply slid away with the greatest of ease. But, by choosing the place where the bats were thickest, we had considerable success, and with each whirl of our bushy sticks several bats would be knocked on to the sandy floor. Then we would drop our weapons and pounce on them before they could regain the air. The knocks they received were not severe, owing to the twigs and leaves on our sticks, but it was sufficient to make them lose control and fall to the floor. Here they would flap their way along the ground, trying hard to get into the air again. Even when in this helpless state they showed a great turn of speed, and it required considerable agility on our part to corner them, and great care in stuffing them into the cloth bags, for their teeth were sharp and very large.

In three-quarters of an hour, during which we vied with the bats in performing strange gyrations round the cave, we had caught twenty-five of these creatures. By now the bats had become wise: some had flown outside, where they hung festooned in the trees like bunches of quivering black fruit, while the others had discovered that if they all crowded to the highest point of the cave's roof they would be safe from us. I decided that twenty-five specimens would be enough to cope with as a beginning, so we called a halt. Some distance from the cave we sat on the ground and enjoyed well-earned cigarettes, and watched the bats dropping from the trees, one by one, and then swooping into the dark interior of the cave to join their chattering companions. It was, in all probability, the first time in the centuries that the colony had lived and bred there that they had been attacked like this. It would probably be the same length of time before they were attacked again. Taking all things into consideration, it must be a pleasant life to lead: all day they sleep, hanging in the dark, cool security of the cave, and then in the evening they awake hungry and fly forth in a great flapping, honking crowd into the light of the setting sun, above the golden tree-tops, to alight and feed in the giant fruit trees aglow with the sunset, gorging on the sweet fruit as the shadows creep through the branches. Chattering and flapping among the leaves, knocking the ripe fruit off so that it falls hundreds of feet down to the forest floor below, to be eaten by other night prowlers. Then, in the faint light of dawn, to fly back to the cave, heavy with food, the fruit juices drying on their fur, to bicker and squabble over the best hanging places, and gradually fall asleep as the sun rises above the trees to ripen a fresh crop of fruit for the next night's feast.

As we left, the shadows were lengthening and I turned for one last look at the cave. It lay like a dark mouth in the cliff face, and as I watched I saw the vanguard of the colony flutter out and soar off high above the trees. Another and another, until a steady stream of bats was pouring forth, like a wisp of smoke at that distance. As we stumbled through the forest in the gloom we could hear them high above us, honking loudly and clearly as they flew off to feed.

CHAPTER FOUR

The Forest by Night

The results of our days spent hunting in the forest, and the prodigious efforts of the villagers for miles around, soon filled my cages to overflowing, and then I found my whole day taken up with looking after the animals. The only time I had for hunting was after the day's work was done, and so it was that we took to hunting at night with the aid of torches. I had brought four great torches out from England with me, and these threw a very strong beam of light. I supplemented our lighting with four more torches purchased on arrival in the Cameroons. Armed with this battery of lights we would scour the forest from midnight to three o'clock in the morning, and by this method we obtained a number of nocturnal beasts which we would otherwise never have seen.

The forest at night was a very different place from the forest by day: everything seemed awake and watchful, and eyes gleamed in the tree-tops above you. Rustles and squeaks came from the undergrowth, and by the light of the torch you could see a creeper swaying and twitching, indication of some movement one hundred and fifty feet above you in the black tree-top. Ripe fruit would patter down on to the forest floor, and dead twigs would fall. The cicadas who never seemed to sleep, would be screeching away, and occasionally a big bird would start a loud "Car . . . carr . . . carr" cry, which would echo through the forest. One of the commonest night noises was caused by an animal which I think was a tree hyrax. It would start off its piercing whistle softly, at regular intervals, then gradually it would work faster and faster until the sounds almost merged, and the whistle would get shriller and shriller. Then, just as it reached a top note and its highest speed, the cry would stop, as though cut short with a knife, leaving the air still quivering with the echoes of the cry. Then there were the frogs and toads: as darkness fell they would start, whistling, hooting, rattling, chirruping and croaking. They seemed to be everywhere, from the tops of the highest trees, to the smallest holes under the rocks on the river banks.

The forest seemed twice as big as normal when you were hunting at night: you moved along under the great, rustling canopy of trees, and outside your torch beam everything was a solid wall of blackness. Only in the small pool of light cast by your torch could you see colour, and then, in this false light, the leaves and the grasses seemed to take on an ethereal silvery-green hue. You felt as though you were moving in the darkest depths of the sea, where there had been no light for a million years, and the pathetically feeble glow of your torch showed up the monstrous curling buttress roots of the trees, and faded the coloration of the leaves, and the silver moths fluttered in groups across the beam, and vanished into the gloom like a silvery school of tiny fish. The air was heavy and damp with dew, and by shining your torch beam upwards, until it was lost in the intricate maze of trunks and branches above, you could see the faint wisps of mist coiling sluggishly through the twigs and creepers. Everywhere the heavy black shadows played you false, making tall slender trees seem to crouch on deformed trunks; the tree roots twisted and writhed as you moved, seeming to slide away into the darkness, so that you could swear they were alive. It was mysterious, creepy, and completely fascinating.

The first night I ventured into the forest with Andraia and Elias we started early, for Elias insisted that we hunted along the banks of a largish river which was some distance from the camp. Here, he assured me, we would find water-beef. What this beast was I had only the haziest notion, for the hunters employed this term with great freedom when discussing anything from a hippo to a frog. All I could get out of Elias was that it was "very fine beef", and that I would be "glad too much" if we caught one. We had progressed about a mile down the path that led into the forest, and we had just left the last of the palm plantations behind, when Elias suddenly came to a halt, and I walked heavily on to his heels. He was shining his torch into the head foliage of a small tree about forty feet high. He walked about, shining his torch from different angles, grunting to himself.

"Na whatee?" I asked, in a hoarse whisper.

"Na rabbit, sah," came back the astonishing reply.

"A *rabbit* . . . are you *sure*, Elias?" I asked in surprise.

"Yes, sah, na rabbit for true. 'E dere dere for up, sah, you no see 'e eye dere dere for stick?"

While I flashed my torch about at the tops of the trees I hastily ran over my knowledge of the Cameroon fauna: I was sure no rabbit had been recorded from the Cameroons, and I was certain an arboreal one had not been recorded from *any* part of the world. I presumed that a rabbit sitting in the top branches of a forty foot tree could be termed arboreal with some justification. Just at that moment two ruby-red spots appeared in my beam: I had located the "rabbit". There, sitting peacefully on a branch high above us, nonchalantly cleaning its whiskers in the torch light, sat a fat grey-coloured rat.

"That's a rat, Elias, not a rabbit," I said, rather pleased to find my zoological knowledge still secure. The appearance of an arboreal rabbit in the zoological world would, I felt, cause rather a stir.

"Na rat, sah? Here we call um rabbit."

"Well, can we catch him, do you think?"

"Yes, sah. Masa and Andraia go wait here, I go climb de stick."

We kept our torches aimed at the rat, and Elias disappeared into the darkness. Presently the tree began to shake as an indication that he had started to climb, and the rat peered downwards in alarm. Then it ran to the end of the small branch it was sitting on and peered down again to get a better view. Elias's head came into view among the leaves directly below the branch on which the rat was sitting. "Which side 'e dere?" he inquired, screwing up his eyes against the light.

"'E dere dere for up, on your left side."

As we shouted our instructions the rat slid down a creeper with great speed and landed on a branch about fifteen feet below Elias.

"'E done run, Elias," screamed Andraia shrilly, "'e dere dere for under you now. . . ."

Painfully, following our shouted directions, Elias descended until he was on a level with the rat. The quarry was still sitting on the branch, putting the finishing touches to his toilet. Slowly Elias edged his way out along the branch towards him, one hand cupped ready to grab. The rat watched him in a supercilious manner, waited until Elias lunged forward, and then launched itself into space. Instinctively we followed it with our torches, and watched it crash into a small bush and disappear. From above came a crack, a roar of anguish and fright, and the sound of a heavy body descending slowly and painfully earthwards. Flashing our torches up we found Elias had disappeared, and only a few leaves fluttered slowly down to show that he had once been up there. We found him nursing his leg in the bushes at the base of the tree.

"Eh . . . aehh!" he groaned, "dat stick no give me chance. It done broke, and I de get wound *plenty*."

Careful examination disclosed only a few scratches, and after soothing Elias's hurt feelings we proceeded on our way.

We had been walking some time and carrying on a lively discussion on the difference between rabbits and rats, when I found we were walking on white sand. Looking up, I discovered that we had left the forest, and above us was the night sky, its blackness intensified by the flickering stars. We were actually walking along the banks of the river, but I had not noticed it, for here the brown waters flowed sluggishly between smooth banks, and so there was no babble of water; the river flowed slowly and silently past us like a great snake. Presently we left the sand beach and made our way to the thick fringe of waist-high growth that formed a border between the sand and the beginning of the forest. Here we paused.

"Na for dis kind of place you go catch water-beef, sah," whispered Elias, while Andraia grunted in agreement. "We go walk softly softly for dis place, and sometime we go find um."

So we commenced to walk softly, softly through the lush undergrowth, shining our torches ahead. I had just paused to pluck a small tree frog from a leaf and push him into the bottle in my pocket, when Elias hurled his torch at me and dived full length into the leaves. In my efforts to catch his torch as it whirled towards me I dropped my own, which hit a rock and promptly went out. I bungled the catch, dropped the second torch as well, and that followed the first into oblivion. Now we only had the illumination of Andraia's, which was very anaemic, for the batteries were damp and old. Elias was rolling about in the undergrowth locked in mortal combat with some creature that seemed frightfully strong. I grabbed the light from Andraia, and in the feeble glow I saw Elias rolling about, and held in his arms, kicking and bucking for all it was worth, was a beautiful antelope, its skin patterned with a lovely pattern of white spots and stripes.

"I done hold um, sah," roared Elias, spitting leaves, "bring flashlamp, sah, quickly, dis beef get power too much. . . ."

I sprang forward eagerly to help him, tripped heavily over a hidden rock and fell on my face. The last torch flickered and went out. I sat up in the gloom and searched frantically for the torch. I could hear Elias desperately imploring someone to help him. Then as my groping fingers found a light, a sudden silence fell. I switched on the torch, after several attempts, and shone it on Elias. He was sitting mournfully on his ample bottom getting leaves out of his mouth. "'E

74

done run, sah," he said. "Sorry too much, sah, but dat beef get power pass one man. Look, sah, 'e done give me wound with his foot." He pointed to his chest, and it was covered with long deep furrows from which the blood was trickling. These had been caused by the sharp, kicking hooves of the little antelope.

"Never mind," I said, mopping his chest with the iodine, "we go catch dis beef some other time."

After a search we found the other two torches, and discovered that both bulbs had been broken by the fall. I had forgotten to bring any spare ones and so our only means of illumination was the third torch, which looked as though it was going to give out at any minute. It was plain that all we could do was to call off the hunt and get back to camp while we still had some means of seeing our way. Very depressed we set off, walking as fast as we could by such a poor light.

As we entered the fields on the outskirts of the village Elias stopped and pointed at a dead branch which hung low over the path. I peered at it hopefully, but it was quite bare, with one dead and withered leaf attached to it.

"Whattee?"

"Dere, for dat dead stick, sah."

"I no see um. . . ."

Disturbed by our whispering the dead leaf took its head out from under its wing, gave us a startled glance, and then flew wildly off into the night.

"Na bird, sah," explained Elias.

It was, altogether, a most unsuccessful night, but it was interesting, and showed me what to expect. The fact that the birds slept so close to the ground amazed me, when there were so many huge trees about in which they could roost. But a little thought showed me why they did this: perched on the end of a long slender twig they knew that, should anything try and crawl along after them, its weight would shake the branch or even break it. So, as long as the branch was long, thin, and fairly isolated, it mattered not if it was a hundred feet up, or five feet from the ground. I questioned Elias closely about this, and he informed me that one frequently came across birds perched as low as that, especially in the farm lands. So the next night, armed with large soft cloth bags, we set out to scour the fields. I was armed with a butterfly net with which to do the actual capturing.

We had not gone far when we found a Bulbul seated on a thin branch about five feet above us, an almost indistinguishable ball of grey fluff against the background of leaves. While the other two kept their torches trained on it, I manœuvred my net into position and made a wild scoop. I don't suppose the Bulbul had ever had such a fright in its life; at any rate it flew off into the darkness tweeting excitedly. It was then I realized that the upward sweeping motion I had employed was the wrong one. So we went a bit further, and presently came across a Pygmy Kingfisher slumbering peacefully. I scooped the net down on him, he was borne to the ground, and within a couple of seconds was in the depths of a cloth bag. Birds, if placed in a dark bag like this, just lie there limp and relaxed, and do not flutter and hurt themselves during transportation. I was thrilled with this new method of adding to my bird collection, as it seemed far superior to the other methods employed. We spent three hours in the fields that night, and during that time we caught five birds: the Kingfisher, two Forest Robins, an Blue-spotted Dove, and a Bulbul. After this, if I was feeling too tired to wander into the forest at night, we would just walk for an hour or so in the fields a mile or two from the camp, and it was rarely that we returned empty-handed.

Elias felt very deeply the loss of the water-beef, and it was not long afterwards that he suggested we should again hunt by the river, mentioning as additional bait, that he knew of some caves in that area. So we set off at about eight o'clock one night, determined to spend all the hours of darkness in pursuit of beef. The night did not start well, for a few miles into the forest we came to the dead stump of a great tree. It had died and remained standing, as nearly all these giants did, until it was hollowed out by insects and the weather into a fine shell. Then the weight of the mass of dead branches at the top was too much, and it snapped the trunk off about thirty feet from the ground, leaving the base standing on its buttress roots like a section of a factory chimney, only much more interesting and aesthetically satisfying. Half-way up this stump was a large hole, and as we passed our torches caught the gleam of eyes from its dark interior. We stopped and held a hasty consultation: as before, Andraia and I kept our torches trained on the hole, while Elias went round the other side of the trunk to see if he could climb up. He returned quickly to say that he was too short to reach the only available footholds, and so Andraia would have to do the

Civet

climbing. Andraia disappeared round the trunk, and shortly after scraping noises and subdued ejaculations of "Eh . . . aehh!" announced that he was on his way up. Elias and I moved a bit closer, keeping our torches steady on the hole. Andraia was two-thirds of the way up when the occupant of the hole showed itself: a large civet. Its black-masked face blinked down at us, and I caught a glimpse of its grey, black-spotted body. Then it drew back into the hole again.

"Careful, Andraia, na bushcat," whispered Elias warningly, for a full-grown civet is the size of a small collie dog.

But Andraia was too busy to answer, for clinging to the bark of the trunk with fingers and prehensile toes was a full-time job. Just as he reached the edge of the hole the civet launched itself out into space like a rocket. It shot through the air, and landed accurately on Elias's chest with all four feet, its weight sending him spinning backwards. As it landed on his chest I saw its mouth open and close, and heard the chop of its jaws. It only missed making its teeth meet in his face because he was already off his balance and starting to fall backwards, and so its jaws missed him by about three inches. It leapt lightly off his prostrate body, paused for one brief moment to stare at me, and then in a couple of swift leaps disappeared into the forest. Elias picked himself up and grinned at me ruefully:

"Eh . . . aehh! Some man done put bad *ju-ju* for dis hunting I tink," he said. "First we lose water-beef next dis bush-cat. . . ."

"Consider yourself lucky you've still got a face left," I said, for I had been considerably shaken by this display of ferocity on the part of the civet, an animal I had always thought was shy and retiring. Just at that moment a strangled yelp came from above us, and we shone our torches up to where Andraia was clinging like a lanky black spider.

"Na whatee?" asked Elias and I together.

"Na something else dere dere for inside," said Andraia shrilly. "I hear noise for inside hole. . . ." He felt in his loin-cloth, and with some difficulty he withdrew his torch and shone it into the hole.

"Eh . . . aehh!" he shouted, "na picken bushcat here for inside."

For a long time Andraia performed the most extraordinary contortions to try and cling on to the tree, while shining the torch into the hole with one hand and endeavouring to insert the other into the hole to catch the baby. At length he succeeded, and his hand came into view holding a spitting, squirming young civet by the tail. Just as he got it out of the hole and was shouting, "Look um, look um," in triumph, the baby bit him in the wrist.

Now Andraia was a complete coward about pain: if he got the smallest thorn in his foot he would put on an exaggerated limp as though he had just had all his toes amputated. So the sharp baby teeth of the civet were like so many hot needles in his wrist. Uttering an unearthly shriek he dropped the torch, the civet, and released his precarious hold on the tree. He, the torch, and the civet crashed earthwards.

How Andraia was not killed by the fall I shall never know: the torch was smashed, and the baby civet landed on its head on one of the iron-hard buttress roots of the tree, and was knocked unconscious. It had a severe haemorrhage about ten minutes later and died without regaining consciousness. Andraia, apart from being severely shaken, was unhurt.

"Eh . . . aehh! Na true some man done put *ju-ju* for us," said Elias again. Whether it was *ju-ju* or not, we were not worried by ill-luck for the rest of the night: on the contrary, we had very good luck. Shortly after our little affair with the civet we came to the banks of a wide stream, about three feet deep in the middle. The water was opaque, a deep chocolate brown colour, and even our torch beams could not pierce it. We had to wade up this stream for about half a mile, until we came to the path on the opposite bank which we were following. Though the surface of the stream was unruffled, there was a considerable undercurrent, and we felt it clutch our legs as we waded in. The water was ice-cold. We had reached the centre and were wading along as swiftly as the deep water and the current would let us, when I became aware that we were not the only occupants of the stream. All around us, coiling and shooting through the dark waters, were dozens of brown water snakes. They swam curiously alongside us, with only their heads showing above water, their tiny eyes glittering in the torch light. Andraia became conscious of the snakes' presence at the same moment, but his reactions were not the same as mine.

"Warr!!" he screamed, and dropping the collecting bag he was carrying, he tried to run for the bank. He had forgotten the water. Here it was almost waist high, and any attempt at running was doomed to failure almost before it was started. As I had anticipated, the strength of the current caught him off his balance, and he fell into the water with a splash that sent every water-snake diving for cover. He surfaced some yards downstream, and struggled to his feet. His lovely sarong, which he had been carefully carrying on his head to protect it, was now a sodden mass.

"Na whatee?" asked Elias, turning round and surveying Andraia, wallowing in the stream like a wounded whale. He, apparently, had not seen the snakes.

"Na snake, Elias," spluttered Andraia, "na snake *too much* for dis water. Why we no fit pass for land?"

"Snake?" asked Elias, shining his torch about the calm waters.

"Na true, Elias," I said, "na water-snake. Andraia de fear too much."

"Eh . . . aehh!" exclaimed Elias wrathfully. "You stupid man, Andraia. You no savvay dis beef no go bite you if Masa be here?"

"Ah!" said Andraia, humbly, "I done forget dis ting."

"What's all this?" I asked. "Why snake no bite Andraia if I'm here?"

Standing in the middle of the stream while Andraia fished about for the collecting bag, Elias explained to me:

"If black man go for water him only, some kind of bad beef, like snake, go smell him, he go come one time and chop him. If black man go for water with white man, de beef smell de white man and he de fear too much, so he no go come."

"Only when we go for water dis ting happen?" I asked. "Yes, sah."

It was a useful piece of knowledge, and I stored it away in my memory for future use. Andraia had by now collected all the things he had dropped, and I suggested that we should turn out the torches and wait to see if the water-snakes returned and, if they did, try to catch some. With a certain lack of enthusiasm my hunters agreed. We stood there in the water, in complete darkness, for about half an hour and then, at a prearranged signal, we all switched on our torches together. All around us were water-snakes, weaving silver patterns in the torchlight. Seizing the net I plunged after the nearest, and after a scramble, managed to get him hissing and wriggling into the net, and from there into the bag. Thus encouraged, Elias and Andraia joined in and within a very short time we had captured twenty of these snakes. But now they were growing wise, and the slightest movement on our part would send them all diving to the murky depths of the river, so we called off the hunt and continued on our way.

I don't know what the attraction of that river was for these snakes, as I never saw them congregated in one spot in such numbers again. Often in the day, and also during our night hunts, we had waded long distances up rivers, but only occasionally had we seen an odd water-snake. In the half-mile we travelled up that stream we saw hundreds of them. It may have been some sort of mating gathering, or maybe a sudden abundance of food in that particular area which had attracted them. We never found out. Some weeks later we crossed the same stream at the same point during the night, and not a snake was to be seen. In places like this you come into contact with many enigmas of this sort, but, unfortunately, you have not the opportunity to investigate as fully as you would like. You can do little more than note them, and wonder about the reason. It is one of the most annoying things about collecting, that you have not the time to investigate these riddles and find an answer, fascinating though that investigation might prove.

We came at last to the place where we had our meeting with the "water-beef", and though we beat the low growth thoroughly, we did not flush another. So we gave it up as a bad job and walked along the sandy banks towards the cliff where Elias said there were some caves. As we rounded the bleached carcass of a huge tree that had fallen across the bank I saw something glowing on the sand ahead of us.

"Elias, na whatee dat?" I asked, pointing.

"Na fire, sah," he replied.

"A fire, out here?"

"Yes, sah, I tink some hunter man sleep here."

As we walked nearer I saw that the glow was caused by

the embers of a small fire. Next to the fire was a tiny, frail lean-to made out of aplings and creepers.

"Ahey!" called Elias, "someone 'e dere dere?"

There was a stirring in the depths of the hut and a black face, sleep-crumpled, peered out at us.

"Na who?" asked the stranger, and I could see he was reaching for his muzzle-loader which lay beside him. Hastily we turned our torches on to ourselves so that he could see who we were.

"Eh . . . aehh!" he gasped. "Na white man dis?"

"Yes," said Elias, "na white man dis."

"What thing white man do for bush for night time?" asked the stranger, and I could see a suspicion dawning on his face that perhaps we were some sort of terrible *ju-ju* in disguise.

"We hunt for beef," said Elias.

I kicked the dying fire into a small flame, sat down beside it and produced cigarettes. The stranger accepted one, but he still kept a hand on his gun.

"Elias," I said, "bring more stick for dis fire, den we get more light, den dis man fit see I be a white man proper and not *ju-ju*." Elias and Andraia laughed, and the man essayed a feeble smile and removed his hand from his gun.

We built up the fire and sat round it smoking, while Elias explained to the man who we were, and what we were doing, and from whence we came. The man, it transpired, was a wandering hunter. These men live in the forest, shooting what they can, and drying the meat. When they have as much as they can manage they trek into the nearest township and sell the meat at the market, buy fresh powder with the proceeds and set off to the bush again. This man had had very good luck, for he had shot four full-grown drills, and he showed us the dismembered bodies, dried by wood smoke. The largest male must have been a magnificent brute in life, and his dried arm, strangely like a mummy's, was knotted with great muscles. His hands and his skull with the flesh dried close to the bone looked decidedly human. We, in our turn, explained what we were doing, and showed the hunter the water-snakes, which he was not enthusiastic over. When we rose to go I dashed him four cigarettes and he, in turn, presented me with a drill leg, saying that it was "very fine chop for white man and black". I ate this leg in a stew, and the hunter was proved correct: it was very fine chop indeed, with a delicate and succulent flavour of beef with the faintest tang of wood smoke about it.

At last we came to the caves: they were in the face of a cliff heavily overgrown with ferns and moss, intermingled with the long creepers that hung down from the trees that grew on the top of the cliff. The usual tumbled mass of boulders littered the base, intergrown with shrubs and bushes. The largest cave was the size of a small room, and from it ran a number of narrow, low tunnels. These, how-ever, were too small to allow us to crawl up them, so we had to content ourselves with lying on our stomachs and shining the torch up in the hopes of seeing something.

Presently we each took a section of the cliff and started a search on our own. I came to another series of these small tunnels, and as I walked along flashing my torch about, something leapt out of the undergrowth ahead and shot into one of them. I hurried to the spot, but I had not much hope of being able to corner whatever it was now that it had gained the sanctuary of its tunnel. Crouching down I shone the torch inside, and discovered that it was a false tunnel, that is to say it ran about eight feet back into the cliff face and then ceased abruptly. The floor of the tunnel was covered with various sized boulders, and the walls were gnarled and full of dark corners and crevices. I could not see the animal, but I presumed that it was hiding somewhere in there as there was, as far as I could see, no exit. Andraia and Elias were some distance away, and I did not like to shout to them to come and help as the more silently one worked the better one's chances of surprising an animal. So I lowered myself to the ground, hung the collecting bag round my neck, put the torch in my mouth, and proceeded to crawl up the tunnel on my stomach. This method is supposed to be the time-honoured one for stalking game, but I found it quite the most painful means of progression known to man. Erosion had given the boulders, which so liberally littered the floor of the tunnel, a razor-like cutting edge to their corners, and most of them had apparently been carefully designed to fit snugly into the more delicate parts of the human anatomy, and thus cause the maximum amount of pain.

I crawled on grimly until I reached the small circular "room" at the end of the tunnel leading off into the depths of the earth. I struggled towards it, and as I reached its mouth a curious sound issued from it, a harsh, rustling rattle, a pause, two thumps, and then silence. I started to crawl closer when the rattling recommenced, a pause, the two thumps were repeated, and then silence. I hastily ran over the list of Cameroon fauna in my mind, but the noise did not seem to belong to anything that I knew of, so I continued my advance with increased caution. Reaching the tunnel I shone my torch inside and found to my surprise that it was also a cul-de-sac, only a much shorter one than the one I was in. As I was flashing my torch round in an effort to see what had produced the noise, there was another burst of rattling, something jumped forward, the torch was knocked out of my hand, and a sharp stinging pain assailed my fingers. I grabbed the torch and backed away hurriedly, and then sat down to examine my hand. On the back of it were a number of spots of blood, and a few deep scratches which now commenced to sting. It looked as though I had plunged my hand into a blackberry bush. I thought about this for a few minutes and then suddenly I realized what it was I had to deal with, one of the commonest animals in the Cameroons, and the only one that could make that noise: a Brush-tailed Porcupine. I was annoyed that I had not thought of it before.

I crawled back, and, with greater care, shone my torch in: there, sure enough, was the porcupine, standing half-turned to me, his spines bristling, and his curious tail rattling like mad. He would give a prolonged rattle on his tail, and then follow it up by stamping his hind feet petulantly, exactly as a rabbit will do when it is scared. He was about the size of a cat, though it was a little difficult to judge accurately, as his erect spines made him look larger. As all his spines pointed backwards he naturally had to stand with his bottom half turned to me, and he peered over his shoulder with his moist black eyes prominent with a mixture of anger and fear. He was mostly black in colour, except for the spines that covered his lower back, which were handsomely patched with black and white. His long tail, which he kept in a U-shape half over his back, was bare of both fur and spines. On its very tip was a curious cluster of spines which had no points: they looked like a head of wheat, pure white, thick and long. It

Brush-tailed Porcupine

was this appendage on his tail which produced the rattling noise, for now and again he would stiffen his tail and rattle these hollow, harmless spines together with a crisp crackling sound. He was all keyed up and alert for trouble.

I began to wonder what to do. It really needed two people to capture him, but even if I enlisted the aid of Andraia or Elias, there was not room in this narrow tunnel for two people. There was nothing for it but to try and capture him myself. So I carefully wrapped my hand in a canvas bag, laid another bag out on the floor in readiness to put him in, and proceeded to crawl cautiously towards him. He rattled and stamped, and uttered shrill squeaks of warning. I manœuvred into position and then suddenly grabbed him by his tail, as this seemed the least protected and most easily handled part of his body. I got it, and immediately he backed with full force on to my hand, and his spines ran straight through the canvas that I had wrapped round as protection, as though it was so much paper. It was extremely painful, but I hung on and dragged him towards me, for I felt that if I let go I might not get another chance to grab him now that he knew my plan of attack. Slowly I wriggled backwards dragging the reluctant porcupine with me, until we were in the small room at the end of the first tunnel. Here there was slightly more room to move, and I tried to get the bag over the animal's head, but he struggled madly, and backed into my chest, the spines going through my thin shirt and well into my flesh. The confined space was in his favour, for whichever way he turned he managed to dig a spine into me, while I had not room to evade his attentions. The only thing to do was to keep on crawling until I reached the open air. So I wriggled along backwards dragging the porcupine, and those last few feet seemed like miles. Just as we reached the open air he gave a terrific bound and a wriggle in an attempt to throw off my hand, but I hung on like grim death. I got shakily to my feet and kept the animal aloft so he could do no damage to me or himself. He hung there quite quietly, all the fight seemed to have gone out of him.

"Andraia . . . Elias . . . come quick, I done catch beef," I called.

They came running, their torches bobbing through the rocks. When they saw what I held they were astonished.

"Na Chook-chook beef," said Elias. "Which side Masa done fine um?"

"Here for dis hole. But he done chop me too much. Get a bag to put him into, my hand done tire."

Elias opened a big canvas bag and I neatly dropped my capture into it. This was my first meeting with a porcupine, and to have captured it single-handed was, I felt, something of a feat.

The Brush-tailed Porcupine, or, as it is known locally, the chook-chook beef, is one of the commonest animals in the

Cameroons: it is found everywhere and in almost every type of country. Most of the faint, twisting paths one found in the forest were the result of the nightly perambulations of this rodent. They would, I found later, make their homes anywhere, but they seemed to favour caves, and particularly caves with small openings under a massive rock, or piles of rocks. In nearly every cave one came across signs of their tenancy: footprints on a sandy floor, a few cast quills, or a half-eaten fruit. In one cave I found fresh palm nuts, which showed that this porcupine in question must have travelled very long distances at night, for the nearest native farm at which he could have obtained this commodity was some six miles away. In another cave I found indications that these porcupines play in much the same way as an English otter will. In this cave there was one wall which was a natural slide, a wall of rock some eight feet high sloping to the ground at a gentle angle of forty-five degrees. This slide had been worn smooth by the constant passage of porcupine bodies or bottoms. Judging by the tracks in the sand, they scrambled up to the top of this slope, slid down, walked round, climbed up again, and slid down once more. They must have been indulging in this game for a number of generations, as the rock-face was worn as smooth as glass. The pidgin-English term for this animal is derived from the word "chook", which means any thorn or spike, and particularly the doctor's hypodermic needle. In pidgin you form the plural of a word by repeating it, so the Brush-tailed Porcupine became naturally the chook-chook beef. I decided that this was a good name for the animal, as I was sore and smarting all over from contact with it. Within two days this specimen had become very tame, and would come to the door of his cage to take fruit from my hand. He would only put up his spines, rattle his tail, and stamp his feet if I put my hand right inside the cage and tried to touch him. Later on he would even come to the bars and let me tickle his ears or scratch a soothing spot under his chin, but this was only allowed if there were bars between us.

After I had finished my smoke and had described in boastful details to my hunters how I had captured the porcupine, we continued on our way. Presently I made another capture, and this made me feel better still: true, it was not such an important specimen as the porcupine, but it was worth while, nevertheless. Clasped tightly to a branch, some ten feet from the ground, my wandering torch beam picked out a pair of sleeping chameleons. They were lying close together, their big eyes closed, their legs tucked carefully in, and body-colour a pale and deceiving silvery-green. We had broken the branch and shaken them into a bag almost before they had woken up and realized what was happening. I presumed, since they were sleeping together like that, that they were either in the process of mating, or had just mated. It turned out that I was right, for some weeks later the female laid five white eggs the size of a sparrow's, in the bottom of her cage.

By the time we had bagged the chameleons I was in such an elated mood that I would have hurled myself unhesitatingly into a single-handed battle with a leopard if one had happened along. Luckily, the great cats in the Cameroons are retiring in the extreme. What did make their appearance in the torch beams, shortly afterwards, was a diminutive pair of galagos or bush-babies. Now there are three species of galago found in the Cameroons, and two of these are rare and have not, to the best of my knowledge, been represented in any zoological collection in England. Accurate identification as to species when an animal is twenty feet above you, and only lit by a torch beam, becomes impossible, so the rule was that any animal remotely resembling a galago was always pursued with determination and vigour. This we proceeded to do with this pair, who were dancing about on some lianas, occasionally looking down at us so that their enormous eyes glowed like outsize rubies. It was definitely a two-man job, so, leaving Andraia to shine the torch on the prey, Elias and I went aloft in different parts of the tree, and started to converge on the animals. They looked not unlike a pair of fluffy grey kittens dancing about from creeper to creeper with a fairy-like grace and lightness, their eyes glowing as they moved. Slowly Elias and I drew nearer, and I manœuvred the butterfly-net into position for capture. After catching two chameleons and a porcupine, I felt that this was going to be child's play. Just as I leant forward to swipe at them, three things happened with startling suddenness: my hand I placed on something long and thin and cold which wriggled vigorously, making me let go of the branch with rapidity, at the same time letting go of the net which sailed downwards to the forest floor. The galagos took fright at this and leapt wildly out into space and disappeared. I crouched very still on my branch for I was not certain of the location of the snake I had leant on, nor was I certain of its species.

"Andraia," I shouted down, "give me some light here. Na snake for dis stick and he go chop me if I no get light."

Andraia moved round and shone the battery of torches at the place where I clung, and I saw the snake. It was coiled round a bunch of twigs and leaves about a foot from my hand. I surveyed it cautiously: the hind end of its body was tangled and twisted round the twigs, but the forequarters were hung forward in the shape of a letter S, apparently ready for action. It was very slender, with a brown skin and darker markings, and a short blunt head furnished with an enormous pair of eyes. It was about two feet long. I watched it, and it watched me, with approximately the same amount of suspicion. I had nothing with which to capture it, except a small length of string which a frantic search through my pockets disclosed. I fashioned a slip-knot out of this and then broke off a large twig to tie my improvised trap to. At this the snake decided to depart, and proceeded to glide through the branches with a fluid rapidity. Hanging on with one hand and my knees, I made three attempts to get the noose over its slender neck, and with the fourth attempt I succeeded. I drew it tight, and the snake hissed and bunched itself into a knot at the end of the string. I tied my handkerchief round the twig to act as a marker and dropped it down to Andraia with instructions. By the time I had reached the ground he had got it safely into a bag. I was extremely annoyed at the loss of the galagos, for we never saw any more specimens in spite of numerous night hunts.

CHAPTER FIVE

The Fossil that Bites

One of the chief charms of collecting is its uncertainty.
One day you will go out loaded down with nets
and bags for the sole purpose of catching bats and
you will arrive back in camp with a python in the nets, your
bags full of birds, and your pockets full of giant millipedes.
You can search for days in the forest after a certain species
of squirrel, and when you have given it up in despair and are
spending a day in camp, a pair of the wretched rodents come
and play among the branches of the tree that overhangs your
tent. Imagine that you can fool fate, and spend a day in the
forest with twenty assistants armed with every conceivable
device for catching anything from an elephant to a fly, and
you will walk all day and see nothing at all. You know that a
certain creature that you want is found only in one type
of country, say in grass fields in the forest. It had never been
recorded in any other type of country by anyone . . . until
you start to look for it. You carefully search every grass field
for miles around, setting traps, smoking, and generally
combing the territory. You catch a remarkable variety of
rats, mice, grasshoppers, snakes, and lizards, in fact everything but the animal you want. But, knowing that it is found
only in grass fields, you persist in your futile task. After you
have searched an acreage that appears to be twice the size of
Argentine pampas you give it up as a bad job, and a week
later you catch your first specimen of the animal sitting in a
thickly overgrown part of the forest, approximately twenty

miles from the nearest grass field. Of course, this sort of thing can be very trying, but as I say, there is a certain charm in sallying forth into the forest and not really knowing whether you will come back empty-handed or with half a dozen of the most priceless specimens you could wish for. There are any number of interesting creatures to be found in the Cameroons, as there are in other parts of the world, and at least half of them have never been seen alive in England, or for that matter, anywhere outside their native forests. There are other creatures which are so rare that they are only known by two or three skins in the museums of the world, and nothing is known about their habits in the wild state. All that is known is that they exist. These sort of specimens were, of course, the ones we wanted most. There are only two ways to find out about how an animal lives, and what its habits are: one is to study it in the wilds and the other is to keep it in captivity. As the greater proportion of zoologists cannot go to outlandish parts of the world to study their specimens in the field, the specimens must be brought to them. That is why I thought it was more important to bring back an animal that had never been seen alive in captivity, even if it was only a species of mouse, than to bother over-much with the larger and better-known animals. Unfortunately, even a collector has to eat, and it is the bigger and more spectacular creatures that command the heavy prices.

There was one inhabitant of the Cameroons which I was more anxious to obtain than any other, and this was the Angwantibo, a small and exceedingly rare lemur, which is found nowhere else in the world except the Cameroon forests. I had been asked especially to try and obtain this creature by the Zoological Society of London, as they had never had a specimen, and it would prove of great interest both to naturalists and anatomists. Of this rare creature I had only one drawing, and this grew gradually more dirty and creased as the days passed, for it was shown to every hunter who came to see me, and I pleaded with them to try and obtain me a specimen. But the weeks rolled by and there was no sign of a specimen, and I began to despair. I raised the price I was offering for it to no avail. As this animal is strictly nocturnal I thought that there was a fair chance of seeing one during our night hunts, and so, whenever possible, I got Elias and Andraia to lead me to parts of the forest where the trees were overgrown with lianas and other parasitic climbing plants, for it was here, as the Angwantibo was arboreal, that I thought we should find one. It was during one of these fruitless hunts for this lemur that we came across a totally different animal but, in its own way, equally rare and interesting.

We had wended our way through miles of forest one night, and climbed up innumerable creeper-enlaced trees without seeing a single living thing. We were seated on the floor having a smoke, all in the deepest depths of depression, when Elias suggested that we should make our way to a stream he knew of some way away, where he felt sure we should catch some baby crocodiles. Feeling that even a baby crocodile would be better than nothing at all as a night's capture, I agreed, and we set off. This night there were four of us: as well as Andraia and Elias there was a youth called Amos, whose duty it was to carry all the bags and nets, thus leaving us all free to shin up a tree at a moment's notice if the need arose. It would be an euphemism to call Amos a half-wit. He seemed to have only the vaguest idea of what we were trying to do, and no amount of argument would convince him that a quiet and orderly progression was necessary to capture, or even see, any animals. He blundered along, dropping tins with an ear-splitting crash, or getting himself and the bags he carried intricately entangled with any bush that he passed. We had, indeed, spent a greater amount of time disentangling him than we had spent searching for beef. I was at the end of my patience and threatened that if he made any more noise or got himself tied up again I would blow his feet off with the shotgun. This threat had the effect of making him giggle uncontrollably for the next half-hour, and fall heavily to the bottom of a small ravine which was full of dead brushwood. His descent sounded reminiscent of a stampeding herd of buffalo.

The stream ran over a bed of granite slabs which the

water had hollowed out into a series of pools and waterfalls. Here and there it had worn grooves in the rock, so that the stream was divided into three or more channels, with ridges of rock between. Occasionally where the stream was level the force of the water had churned up the white sand into small banks that glistened like ivory in the torchlight. Stopping on the bank we cut ourselves forked sticks, and then waded into the water and proceeded upstream. Half an hour of this and suddenly a pair of fiery eyes glowed on a small sandbank ahead. We moved forward cautiously and discovered a small crocodile, about eighteen inches long, lying there, his head raised alertly as he watched our approach. We kept the torches aimed at his eyes and crept forward until we were near enough to pin him down by the neck with our forked

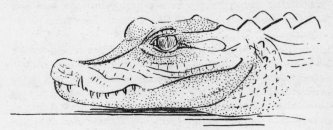

Broad-fronted Crocodile

sticks. Then I picked him up and, after considerable argument with Amos, who had retreated rapidly with the gear, I put him safely in a box. We moved on, our gloom lessened by this capture, and came to a wall of rock some twenty feet high, over which the waters of the stream tumbled in a foaming torrent. The surface of the rock face was moist, overgrown with ferns and begonias. With great care we started to climb, and half-way up, as I was intrepidly edging my way along a narrow ledge above the fall, I perceived a fat and beautiful toad squatting under a bunch of ferns. It was a vivid mustard yellow, and it sat there gazing at me in the vacant way that toads have, breathing rapidly. I had never seen a toad of that colour before, and I was grimly determined that I would add him to the collection. It was not, however, as easy as it appeared, for I was standing on a very narrow ledge and clinging to the rock face by my finger-tips. The surface of the rock, as I say, was so slippery that I had to exercise the utmost caution in moving, or I would crash ten feet into the pot-holes below the falls, where the black waters swirled and foamed vigorously. I looked up and found that Elias had reached the top of the falls and was now squatting above me, lighting my progress with his torch.

"Elias," I called, "na beef for here, but I no get chance to catch um. Give me one end of your cloth, then I get something to hold, and I fit catch um. . . ."

Elias at once unwound the cloth from his waist and, holding on to one end, lowered the other down to me. It was far too short. I cursed myself for not having brought any rope.

"Get Andraia's cloth and tie the two together," I instructed.

A frenzied argument broke out as I waited. Apparently Andraia was a modest man and did not relish the idea of standing on the top of a waterfall stark naked. At length the cloths reappeared, with a large knot in the middle. I took hold of them and was thus able to release one hand for the purpose of capturing the toad. I then discovered that this creature, while my attention was engaged, had hopped along a ledge, and was now about six feet away from me. Hanging on to the cloth I edged after him. He had perched himself at a place where the cliff bulged out, so that I was compelled to hang out over the waters, almost my entire weight being supported by the cloth. Offering up a brief prayer I made a wild grab and caught the toad by the hind leg. The movement of my grab swung me out in an arc over the pool below, and instinctively I looked upwards to make sure all was well at the top. To my horror I saw the large knot which joined the two cloths start to disintegrate. I reached my former position just as the cloths parted. Andraia, peering over the edge, was treated to the sight of his cloth whizzing merrily round and round the miniature whirlpool below.

When we had all reached the top safely, after rescuing

Andraia's cloth, I sat down to examine the toad. My feelings can be imagined when I found that my rare specimen was, in reality, the commonest form of toad in the Cameroons, one who had changed his normal colour for this bright livery because the breeding season was near. I released him sadly, and watched him hop off into the undergrowth with slow measured leaps, and an astonished look on his face.

We moved along the stream, which now flowed a broken and foam-whitened course between large boulders, keeping a hopeful look-out for more crocodiles. Presently we succeeded in catching two more. Then we waded for an hour and saw nothing. Once a pair of eyes gleamed for a brief second in a tree above us, but we could not find their owner when we searched. Amos had now become tired and waded far behind, uttering at intervals a loud mournful groan. I knew that this was not a complaint, only his way of keeping his spirits up, but it annoyed me none the less, and my mind was filled with dark thoughts of what I would like to do to him. Elias and Andraia were wading ahead, and I followed carrying their forked sticks, thus leaving their hands free to manœuvre the torches. Soon, as we had not seen a living thing for what seemed hours, I did a very silly thing: in a fit of exasperation I threw the sticks away, thinking that we could always cut more should the need arise. Not long afterwards Elias came to a sudden halt and, keeping the torch beam steady on something he had seen, he groped behind him with his free hand and implored me to hand him his stick. I replied that I had lost them.

"Eh . . . aehh!" muttered Elias in righteous indignation, and he drew his machete and crept forward; I peered to see what it was that he was stalking, and saw something long and dark lying on the sandbank ahead, something which was the size and shape of a small crocodile and which glinted in the light like one. Elias crept near, and then made a sudden dive, trying to pin it to the sand with his machete blade, but it wriggled through his legs, plopped into the water and swam at great speed towards Andraia. He jumped at it as it passed, but it put on a spurt of speed and shot towards me like a miniature torpedo. By now I was convinced it was a crocodile, so, waiting until it came level I flung myself into the water on top of it. I felt its body give a convulsive wriggle against my chest, but as I grabbed at it, it slid through my fingers like oil. Now no one stood in its path to freedom except Amos. Elias, Andraia, and I lifted up our voices and yelled instructions to him. He stood there with his mouth open, watching its approach. It was level with him, churning a small wake in the stream, and then it was past him and making for the sanctuary of a tangle of boulders and still he stood and watched it.

"Arrrrr!" roared Elias. "You blurry fool, you. Why you no catch um?"

"I see um," said Amos suddenly, "he go for under dat stone. . . ."

The three of us rushed down towards him in a tidal wave of foam and water, and Amos pointed out the rock under which the quarry was lurking. This was by the bank, in shallow water, and under it was the hole in which the creature had taken refuge. Elias and Andraia, in their eagerness, both bent down at the same time to examine this hole, and banged their heads together with a resounding clump. After a short pause for abuse, Andraia bent down and pushed his hand into the hole to see how large it was. The creature had apparently been waiting for such a move, for he withdrew his hand with a cry of anguish, his forefingers dripping blood.

"This beef can bite man," said Elias, with the air of having made a discovery.

Andraia was at last persuaded, since he had the longest arm, to put his hand back in the hole and drag out the beef by force, but not before he and Elias had had a long and shrill altercation with each other in Banyangi, and accusations of cowardice had been made and indignantly denied. Andraia lay down on his tummy in six inches of water and insinuated his hand into the bowels of the earth, explaining all the time how clever he was to do this. Then there was a short silence, broken only by his frenzied grunts in his efforts to reach the beast. Suddenly he gave a yell of triumph, scrambled to his feet dripping with water, and holding the beast by its tail.

Now, up to that moment, I had been convinced that we were attempting the capture of yet another baby crocodile, so as I gazed at the creature which now hung from his hand I received a considerable shock. For there, dangling in the torchlight, sleek and angry, hissing like a snake out of a quivering maze of whiskers, was a full-grown Giant Water Shrew, an animal that I had never expected to find. I could do nothing intelligent, I just stood there gazing at this fabulous creature with my mouth open. The shrew, however, got tired of hanging by his tail, so he turned and climbed up his

Giant Water Shrew

own body with sinewy grace, and buried his teeth in Andraia's thumb. The proud hunter leapt wildly into the air and uttered an ear-splitting scream of pain: "Ow!... Ow! ... Ow!..." he screamed, wagging his hand in an effort to dislodge the shrew. "Oh, Elias, Elias, get it off.... Ow!... My JFSUSCRI'... it done kill me.... Ow!... Ow!... Ow! ... Elias, quickly!" Elias and I struggled with the shrew to make it let go, but it seemed quite content to hang there, occasionally tightening its jaws to show it was still taking part in the contest. After prolonged effort, during which Andraia nearly deafened us with his cries of pain and calls for aid to the Almighty, we succeeded in prising the shrew loose, and dropped it, hissing and wriggling, into a canvas bag. Then I examined Andraia's hand: the whole first joint of his thumb was a mass of blood, and when I had washed this away I found that he had been badly mangled by the creature's teeth. It had bitten through the ball of his thumb right down to the bone, the flesh was hanging off in strips, and the wounds were bleeding profusely. I decided that we should return home, partly owing to Andraia's thumb, which must have been exceedingly painful, and also because I wanted to get my new specimen into a decent cage as soon as possible. So we walked swiftly back to the village, the groans emitted by Amos and Andraia giving the whole trek the air of a funeral procession rather than a triumphant home-coming.

While I changed out of my wet clothes Elias went down to the village and roused the Carpenter from his bed, and then we set to work to fashion a cage fine enough to house this rarity. The sky was a pale green flecked with the red of coming dawn as we drove in the last nail, then I tenderly undid the sack and gently shook the Giant Water Shrew into his new home. He sat there for a minute, wiffling his mass of whiskers, and then slid swiftly through the hole into his darkened bedroom. I could hear him rustle round once or twice among the dry banana leaves inside, and then came a deep sigh and silence. The Water Shrew was taking his capture very quietly. I did not emulate him: the entire staff was marshalled to go down to the river and catch me fish, frogs, water-snakes, and crabs; and two carriers were hastily dispatched into Mamfe to procure an empty drum to act as a swimming pool for the Shrew. While all this was taking place I kept creeping back to his cage every five minutes to see if there was any sign of life. Soon I had a basket full of crabs, six frogs, ten fish, and a rather anaemic-looking water-snake. Arranging all these within easy reach I started to feed the Shrew.

After my banging on his bedroom door for a bit he condescended to come out into the open part of his cage, and as the sun was now up I had my first real good look at him. He was nearly two feet long, of which more than half was composed

of his tail. This strong muscular member was not flattened
from top to bottom as an otter's is, but from side to side like
a tadpole's. The hair on it was so short and sleek that it
looked as though the whole tail was made out of polished
black leather. All the top half of the animal was black, but
paws, belly, throat and chest were pure white. The body was
small and dumpy, and the head curiously flattened. Its
muzzle and parts of its cheeks near the nose were swollen
and enlarged, and from this bristled a forest of stiff white
whiskers. From on top, the Shrew's head looked not unlike
the head of a hammer. Its feet were small and neat, and its
eyes were microscopic pin-points of glinting jet buried in the
fur.

I opened the door of its cage and threw the snake in. The
Shrew approached it, preceded by its quivering mass of
whiskers. The snake made a slight movement, the Shrew
sniffed, and then backed rapidly away, hissing furiously in
the same way I had noticed before. I removed the snake and
tried a frog, with the same results. Then I tried a fish which,
according to the earliest reports on this animal, is its only
food, and the Shrew refused that as well. He was rapidly getting bored with these proceedings, and was casting hopeful
looks at his bedroom, when I threw in a large crab. He approached, sniffed, and then, before the crab had time to get
his pincers ready, the Shrew had overturned it and delivered
a sharp bite through the underside, almost cutting the crab
in two with one bite. Having done this, he then settled down
and finished off his meal with great rapidity, scrunching
loudly and quivering his whiskers. Within half an hour he
had polished off four crabs, and so his feeding problem was
settled for the moment.

The next day the carriers returned from Mamfe staggering under the weight of a huge petrol drum. This had to
be cut in half, lengthways, all the rust scraped out, and any
trace of oil removed by boiling water in it for twenty-four
hours. Then the Shrew was removed from his cage while a
sliding door was fitted in the bottom. The whole cage was
then placed on top of the half petrol drum; thus, by opening

and closing the sliding door I could let the Shrew in and out of his private bathing pool. He enjoyed this immensely, and every night made the most resounding hisses and grunts in its hollow interior while in pursuit of his crab dinner. I found that the water fouled very quickly, so that it had to be changed three times a day, much to the water-boy's annoyance. The Shrew, now adequately housed and with access to water, settled down very well and proceeded to demolish twenty or twenty-five crabs a day, which proved lucrative for the small boys who collected them.

The Giant Water Shrew is perhaps one of the most interesting animals to be found in West Africa. It is, to all intents and purposes, a living prehistoric creature, a warm blooded, breathing, biting fossil. *Potomagale velox*, as it is called scientifically, was first discovered by Du Chaillu, the gentleman who brought such discredit upon himself by his lurid accounts of gorilla-hunting in the eighteen-hundreds. Owing to his penchant for colouring his material with the aid of a fertile imagination, Du Chaillu's every statement or discovery became suspect in the eyes of zoologists. However, in the case of *Potomagale* he seems to have contented himself with repeating just what the natives told him, and so in his original description he endows it with habits and a choice of food which appear to be completely wrong.

The animal has no relatives in the world, except a small mouse-like creature called *Geogale*, which lives in Madagascar. As it is unknown in fossil form it is impossible to say exactly how old an animal *Potomagale* is, but we do know that it comes from an ancient lineage, for ages ago in the earth's history, at a time known to geologists as the Cretaceous Period, there lived an animal which is called by the jaw-breaking name of *Palaeoryctes*. It is the earliest insectivore known to science, and must have been a forerunner of the *Potomagale's* family, for their teeth are almost identical, except that the *Potomagale's* are much larger. So the Giant Water Shrew can trace his family back to a period in the world's history before man was even known, in his present shape, on earth. He has also one other peculiarity which makes him

distinct from all other insectivores, and thus more aristo-
cratically sure of his uniqueness: he does not have collar-
bones!

My thought now turned to a very important matter: what
was I going to give him to eat on the long voyage home?
True, I could take a supply of live crabs with me, but even
then these would run out eventually, and there was no supply
of freshwater crabs in England that I knew of. The only
thing was to get him on to a substitute food, and my heart
sank at the thought. Then I remembered that the natives in
the Cameroons catch the fresh water-shrimps, dry them in
the sun, and sell them in the markets as a delicious addition
to groundnut or palm oil chop, or, for that matter, any other
dish. I decided that these would have to be the substitute
for the crabs, so a member of the staff was sent to the nearest
market to procure several pounds of this product. Using
these small, biscuit-dry shrimps as a base, I mixed in raw
egg and some finely chopped meat. Then I got two large
crabs, killed them, scooped out their insides and proceeded
to stuff them with this rather nauseating mess. Having prepared them I went to the Shrew's cage and threw him a small,
live, and unstuffed crab, which he soon demolished, and then
started to look round for more. Then I threw in a stuffed
crab, and he fell on it and proceeded to scrunch it avidly.
After the first few bites he paused, sniffed suspiciously (while
I held my breath), and then stared at it for a minute. But, to
my delight, he fell to again and demolished the lot.

Gradually I weaned him on to this new diet until he was
eating it out of a dish, and having four or five crabs as dessert,
and he thrived on it. I was getting prepared to show him off
to John on arrival at Bakebe, and even making up boastful
speeches on how easy it was to keep a Giant Water Shrew in
captivity, when the object of my love suddenly died. He was
fat, and in the best of spirits one night, and the next morning
he was dead. As I sadly consigned his body to the formalin
bottle I reflected that it was probably the only chance I
would ever get of keeping one of these fascinating creatures
alive.

Another one of the unwritten rules of collecting, however, seems to be that you may go to endless trouble to get your first specimen, but, once having got it, the others follow thick and fast. So, some time later, I was pleased, but not unduly surprised, when a youth wandered into the compound carrying a wicker fish-trap, inside of which crouched a lovely young Giant Water Shrew. It was a female and could not have been more than a few months old, for she measured about twelve inches with her tail, against the two feet of the adult I had captured. I was very elated with this arrival, for I thought that, being a young specimen, she would settle down to captivity and a substitute diet in a more satisfactory manner than an adult. I was perfectly right, for within twenty-four hours she was eating the substitute food, snorting like a grampus in her bathing pool, and even allowing me to scratch her behind the ears, a liberty I could not have taken with the adult. For a month she lived happily in her cage, feeding well, and growing rapidly. I was confident that she was to be the first Giant Water Shrew to arrive in England. But, as if to warn me against undue optimism, and to prove that collecting is not as easy as it sometimes seems, fate stepped in, and one morning on going to the cage I found my baby Shrew dead. She had apparently died in the same mysterious way as the adult, for she had seemed as lively as usual the night before, when I had fed her, and she had eaten a good meal.

The Giant Water Shrew was really the zenith of our night-hunting results. Short of getting an Angwantibo (an animal which by now I was coming to look upon as an almost mythical beast!), we could not have beaten it as a capture. For weeks after every waterway for miles around was filled with hunters who, spurred on by the price I had offered, were determined to get me another Shrew. But they had no luck, and after two weeks of intensive night hunts, during which I wore myself out looking for Shrews and Angwantibos, I had to give up night hunting and confined my attentions to the camp, where the ever growing collection provided me with quite enough work.

CHAPTER SIX

Beef and the Bringers of Beef

★

The camp site was a rectangular area hacked out of the thick undergrowth on the edge of the forest. Fifty feet away a small stream had carved itself a valley in the red clay, and it was on the edge of the valley that the camp was situated. My tent was covered with a palm-leaf roof for extra protection, and next door to this was the animal house, a fairly large building constructed out of palm-leaf mats on a framework of rough wood saplings, lashed together with forest creepers. Opposite was the smaller replica which served as a kitchen and behind some large bushes, was the hut in which the staff slept.

It had taken considerable time and effort to arrange this camp just as I wanted it. At one time there had been three separate gangs of men building different houses, and the noise and confusion was terrible. The whole area was knee deep in coiling creepers, palm mats, boxes of tinned food, wire traps, nets, cages, and other equipment. Africans were everywhere, wielding their machetes with great vigour and complete disregard for human life. Through this chaos came a steady trickle of women, some old and withered with flat dugs and closely shaven grey heads, smoking stubby black pipes; some young and plump with shining bodies and shrill voices. Some brought food to their husbands, some brought calabashes full of frogs, beetles, crabs, and catfish, specimens they had caught while down at the river, and which they thought I might buy.

"Masa . . . Masa," they would call, waving a calabash full of clicking, bubble-blowing crabs, "Masa go buy dis ting? Masa want dis kind of beef?"

At first, with no cages ready for the reception of specimens, I was forced to refuse all the things they brought. I was afraid that, as I had to do this, they would become disgruntled and give up bringing animals; I need not have worried: some women returned with the same creatures three and four times a day to see if I had changed my mind.

Before accepting any creatures I wanted to get the camp site more or less organized, and then I had to get down to the construction of cages to house the animals. With this end in view I engaged a man who had once been a carpenter, and he squatted down with a great pile of broken boxes in the middle of the camp and proceeded to work quickly and well, undeterred by the noise and upheaval around him. Soon my stock of cages had grown, and I felt I was then in a position to deal with any eventuality, so the message went whispering around the village that Masa was now buying animals, and the trickle of beef bringers swelled into a flood, a flood that threatened to overwhelm both the carpenter and me. Sometimes we would be working by the light of hurricane lamps until two and three in the morning, hurrying to finish a cage, while near us, on the ground, would lie a row of sacks and bags, each heaving and twitching with the movement of its occupant.

The Bringers of Beef were divided into three categories: the children, the women, and the hunters. From the children I would get such things as palm spiders, great brown palm weevils, various types of chameleon, and the lovely silver and brown forest skinks. From the women I would get crabs, both land and river, frogs and toads, water-snakes, an occasional tortoise, a few fledgeling birds, and the great whiskered catfish from the muddy river. It was the hunters who brought the really exciting specimens: mongoose, brush-tailed porcupine, squirrels, and other rarer inhabitants of the deep forest. The children preferred to be paid in the big shiny West African penny, with a hole through its middle;

the women preferred to be paid half in salt, and half in shillings; and the hunters would take nothing but cash payments. They fought shy of accepting paper money and would prefer to carry away a couple of pounds in pennies rather than accept a note. And so they came, from the tiny youngsters who could only just walk, to the oldest man or woman hobbling to the camp with the aid of a stick, each carrying some living creature, either in a calabash, or a sack, tied to a stick, or in a neat wicker basket. Some arrived stark naked and unembarrassed, their contribution wrapped in their loincloth. Every box and basket was pressed into commission as a cage, every empty kerosene tin was washed and cleaned, and soon contained a mass of vacant-faced frogs, or a tangled knot of snakes. Bamboo cages full of birds hung everywhere, and monkeys and mongooses were tethered to every post and stump. The collection was really under way.

One morning, bright and early, I was shaving outside the tent, when a large and scowling man made his appearance carrying a palm-leaf bag on his back. He strode forward, dumped the bag at my feet, and stood back glowering silently at me. I called Pious, who was in the kitchen supervising the cooking of breakfast.

"Pious, what has this man brought?"

"Na what kind of beef you get dere?" Pious asked the man.

"Water-beef."

"He say it water-beef, sah," said Pious.

"What's a water-beef? Have a look, Pious, while I finish shaving."

Pious approached the bag and carefully cut the string round its mouth. He peered inside.

"Crocodile, sah. It very big one," he said, "but I tink it dead!"

"Is it moving?" I inquired.

"No, sah, it no move at all," said Pious, and proceeded to shake four and a half feet of crocodile out on to the ground. It lay there, limp as it is possible for a crocodile to be, with its eyes closed.

"It dead, sah," said Pious, and then he turned to the man. "Why you go bring dead beef, eh? Why you no take care no wound um, eh? You tink sometime Masa go be foolish an' he go pay you money for dead beef?"

"Water-beef no be dead," said the hunter.

"No be dead, eh?" asked Pious in wrath. "Na whatee dis, eh?" He flicked the crocodile with the bag: it opened both eyes, and suddenly came to life with unbelievable speed. It fled through Pious's legs, making him leap in the air with a wild yelp of fright, dashed past the hunter, who made an ineffectual grab at it, and scuttled off across the compound towards the kitchen. Pious, the hunter, and myself gave chase. The crocodile, seeing us rapidly closing in on him, decided that to waste time going round the kitchen would be asking for trouble, so he went straight through the palm-leaf wall. The cook and his helpers could not have been more surprised. When we entered the kitchen the crocodile was half through the opposite wall, and he had left havoc behind him. The cook's helper had dropped the frying-pan with the breakfast in it all over the floor. The cook, who had been sitting on an empty kerosene tin, overbalanced into a basket containing eggs and some very ripe and soft pawpaw, and in his efforts to regain his feet and vacate the kitchen he had kicked over a large pot of cold curry. The crocodile was now heading for the forest proper, with bits of curry and wood ash adhering to his scaly back. Taking off my dressing-gown I launched myself in a flying tackle, throwing the gown over his head, and then winding it round so tight that he could not bite. I was only just in time, for in another few yards he would have reached the thick undergrowth at the edge of the camp. Sitting in the dust, clutching the crocodile to my bosom, I bargained with the man. At last we agreed to a price and the crocodile was placed in the small pond I had built for these reptiles. However, he refused to let go of my dressing-gown, of which he had got a good mouthful, and so I was forced to leave it in the pond with him until such time as he let it go. It was never quite the same again after its sojourn in the crocodile pool. Some weeks later another crocodile escaped and did precisely the same thing, horrifying the kitchen staff, and completely ruining my lunch. After this, all crocodiles were unpacked within the confines of the pool, and at least three people had to be on hand to head off any attempts at escape.

Some time after this another arrival created excitement of a different sort. I had been working late on cage building, and at length climbed into bed about twelve o'clock. About an hour later I was awakened by an uproar from the direction of the village. Shrill cries and screams, the clapping of hands, and ejaculations of "Eh . . . aehh!" came to me clearly. Thinking that it was the prelude to yet another dance, I turned over and tried to get to sleep again. But the noise persisted and steadily grew louder. Lights flickered among the trees, and I could see a great crowd of people approaching from the direction of the village. I scrambled out of bed and clothed myself, wondering what on earth could have brought such a mass of humanity to disturb me at that hour of night. The crowd poured into the compound and it seemed as though practically the whole village was there. In the centre of this milling, gesticulating crowd walked four men carrying on their backs an enormous wicker basket, shaped somewhat like a gigantic banana. They dropped this at my feet, and as if by magic the great crowd fell silent. A man stepped forward, a tall, ugly fellow clad in the tattered remains of a khaki tunic and an enormous dirty sola topee. He swept me a low bow. "Masa," he began grandiloquently, "I done bring you fine beef. I bring Masa best beef Masa get for dis country. I be fine hunter, I no get fear, I go to bush and I de see dis beef for hole. Dis beef get plenty power, Masa, but 'e no get power pass me. . . . I be very strong man, I get plenty power, I . . ."

He was at a disadvantage. I disliked his pseudo-civilized garb, and I also disliked the lecture on himself he was delivering. Also I was tired and eager to see the specimen, strike a bargain, and get back to bed.

"Listen, my friend," I interrupted him, "I see dat you be very fine hunter man, and that you get power pass bush cow. But I want to know wnat kind of beef you get first, you hear?"

"Yes, sah," said the man abashed. He dragged the great basket into the lamplight so that I could see it.

"Na big big snake, sah," he explained, "na boa."

Inside the basket, completely filling the interior, was one of the biggest pythons I had ever seen. It was so large that they had been unable to fit all of it inside, and so about three feet of its tail was outside, strapped tightly with creepers to the side of the basket. It fixed me with its black and angry eyes through the wickerwork, and hissed loudly. I contemplated his great length, coiled in the basket, his glossy, coloured skin shining in the lamplight.

"Listen, my friend," I said to his owner, "I no get chance for look dis fine beef to-night. You go leave de beef here, and you go come back for morning time. Den we go look de beef and we go make palaver for price. You hear?"

"Yes, sah," said the hunter. With the aid of the spectators we carried the heavy basket into the animal house and laid it on the floor. I emptied two buckets of water over the snake, for I was sure it must be very thirsty. Then I cut the ropes that tied the tail to the basket. These had been pulled so tight that they had, in places, cut into the lovely skin. I rubbed the tail for a time to try and restore the circulation that must have been checked by these tight bonds. Then I shooed the villagers out of the compound and retired once more to bed.

In the morning I examined the python, and as far as I could judge it seemed undamaged, though very cramped by the size of the basket, which appeared to have been built round the reptile after capture. After a long bargaining session, which lasted all through breakfast, I at length bought it at my price, and then the question of caging arose. I chose the largest box I could find, and the carpenter was detailed to do a rush job converting it for the snake. By lunch time the cage was ready and filled with a thick layer of dried banana leaves to give the python a soft bed to lie on. Then came the question of getting him out of the basket and into the box.

Now, ordinarily, if you have a few trustworthy men to help you, the moving of a python of any size is simple. Someone grabs the head, someone the tail, and the others hold on to various bits of his body. Keep him well stretched out so that he has no chance to coil round anything, and he is comparatively helpless. All I lacked was the few trustworthy men. To the Africans the python is a poisonous snake, and does not only poison you with his tongue, but with the sharp point of his tail as well. Useless for me to protest that I would hold the head, while they held the harmless parts of his anatomy. They would point out that they could easily be killed by the tail. I had no particular desire to get the python out of his basket and then have my helpers suddenly let go and leave me on my own to subdue his great length. After a prolonged argument I got angry.

"Listen," I said, "if this snake is not inside that box in half an hour no one will get any pay."

So saying, I cut through the side of the basket, grabbed the python firmly round the neck, and proceeded to pull him out, yard by yard. As each length of him was pulled out of the basket reluctant black hands took hold of it. Holding his head in one hand I waited for his tail to come into view, and then I grabbed it. Thus the python was now stretched in a circle: I held his head and his tail, and a ring of frightened Africans held gingerly on to his wriggling body. Then I thrust his tail into the box, and we gently eased his body after it, foot by foot. When it was all inside I pushed his head in, let go quickly, and slammed the door shut and sat on it with a sigh of relief. The staff were very excited at their own bravery and stood around showing each other how they had held it, what it had felt like, and what a great weight it was and so on. I sent one of them down to the village to purchase a chicken, for I felt that the reptile might be hungry, and when it arrived I placed it with the snake. During the night it ate the fowl and I thought it was going to be all right. Then came one of those twists that make collecting so difficult: the python's tail, which had been tied up so tightly and for so long, developed gangrene. This is the danger of tying up any creature too tightly even in a cool climate, but in the tropics gangrene develops and spreads with ferocious rapidity. Within ten days there was nothing I could do for the reptile: it was feeding well, but the condition of its tail got worse, in spite of antiseptic treatment. Very reluctantly I was forced to put it out of its misery. Stretched out, it measured eighteen and a half feet in length. On dissection it proved to be a female with some half-developed eggs inside. I never saw a python that size alive again, and I was never brought another even approaching that size.

The general impression of collecting seems to be that you have only to obtain an animal, stick it in a cage, and the job is done. As a rule it means that the job has only just begun: to locate and capture a specimen may be hard, but it pales into insignificance in comparison with the task of finding it a suitable substitute food, getting it to eat that food, watching to see that it does not develop some disease from close confinement, or sore feet through constant contact with wooden boards. All this in addition to the daily routine of cleaning and feeding, seeing they get neither too much sun nor too little, and so on. There are some creatures who simply will not eat on arrival, and hours have to be spent devising titbits to try and tempt them. Sometimes with this sort of specimen you are lucky, and by experiment you discover something which it likes. But in some cases they will refuse everything, and then the only thing to do is to release the creatures back into the forest. In some cases, which were fortunately rare, you could neither satisfy the animal's palate, nor could you release it: these cases were the very young specimens. The very worst of these in my experience were the baby duikers.

The duikers are a collection of antelope found only in Africa. They range from the size of a fox-terrier to the size of a St. Bernard, and in colour from a pale slaty blue to a rich fox-red. It was the latter species of duiker which seemed exceedingly common around Eshobi. During the time I was there it was apparently the breeding season for this duiker, and the hunters out shooting were always finding the young in the forest, or else shooting a female to find that she had been accompanied by her baby. Then the baby was caught and brought to me. Apropos of this I would like to point out that the protection laws for animals in the Cameroons do not take into consideration the breeding season of any animal, so that the hunter is within his rights to kill a female with young. To him this is a windfall, for he not only gets the mother but the youngster as well, and this without wasting any gunpowder on it. Judging by the number of babies that were brought to me, the annual slaughter during the breed-

Ogilby's Duiker (Adult)

ing season must be considerable and, although this species of duiker seems very common at the moment, one wonders how long they will remain so.

When the first duiker was brought to me I purchased it, constructed a suitable cage, and felt very elated at this beautiful addition to the collection. Very soon I realized that these duiker were going to be more difficult than any deer or antelope I had previously dealt with. For the first day the

baby would not eat anything, and was very nervous. The
next day it realized that I was not going to hurt it and then
started to follow me around like a dog, gazing up at me
trustfully out of its great, dark, liquid eyes. But it still refused the bottle. I tried every trick I knew to get it to drink:
I bought an adult duiker skin and draped it over a chair, and
when the baby nosed round it, presented the nipple of the
bottle from under the skin. The baby would take a few half-
hearted sucks, and then wander off. I tried hot milk, warm
milk, cold milk, sweet milk, sour milk, bitter milk, all to no
purpose. I put a string around its neck and took it for walks
in the adjacent forest, for it was just at the age when it could
be weaned, and I hoped that it might come across some leaf
or plant that it would eat. We walked round and round, but

Ogilby's Duiker (Young)

the only thing it did was to scratch a small hole in the leafy
floor and lick up a little earth. Day by day I watched it getting weaker, and I tried desperate measures: it was held
down and forced to drink, but this process frightened it so
much in its weakened condition that it was doing more harm
than good. In desperation I sent the cook off to the nearest
town to try and buy a milking goat. Goats are not so easy to
come by in the forest areas, and it was three days before he
returned. By this time the baby was dead. The cook had
brought with him the most ugly and stupid goat it had ever
been my misfortune to come into contact with, a beast that
proved to be absolutely useless. During the three months we
had her she gave, very reluctantly, about two cupfuls of
milk. At the sight of a baby duiker she would put her head

down and try to charge it. It required three people to hold her while the baby drank. In the end she was consigned to the kitchen, where she provided the main ingredients for a number of fine curries.

Still the baby duikers were brought in, and still they refused to eat, wasted, and died. At one time I had six of these beautiful little creatures wandering forlornly around the compound, occasionally uttering a long drawn-out, pathetic, "barrrrr", exactly like a lamb. Each time that one arrived on the end of a string I swore that I would not buy it, but when it nuzzled my hand with its wet nose, and turned its great dark eyes on me, I was lost. Perhaps, I would think, this one will be different: perhaps it will drink, and so I would buy it, only to find it was the same as all the others. Six baby duikers wandering around the camp bleating hungrily, and yet refusing everything that was offered, was not the sort of thing to raise anyone's spirits, and at length I called a halt to the purchase of them. I realized that they would be consigned to the cook-pot of the hunter if I did not buy them, but I felt that this was at least a quick death in comparison to the gradual wasting away. I shall never forget the long and depressing struggle I had with these little antelope: the hours walking in the forest, leading them on strings, trying to tempt them to eat various leaves and grasses, the long wet struggle with the bottle, both the baby and myself dripping milk, but only the smallest amount going down its throat; crawling out of bed at three in the morning to repeat this dampening process, half asleep, the babies struggling and kicking, tearing my pyjamas with their sharp little hooves. The gradually weakening legs, the dull coats, their big eyes sinking into their sockets, and growing dim. It was by this experience more than any other that I learnt that collecting is not as easy as it appears.

It was during the time that I was suffering the trials and tribulations of duiker rearing that I engaged what in the Cameroons is known as Watchnight. It was my first introduction to this fraternity, and throughout my time in the Cameroons I suffered much at their hands. There were two reasons for engaging a night watchman: the first was that I needed someone to put the kettle on and heat the water for the night feed of the duikers, and then to wake me up. The second, and more important reason, was that he patrolled the edge of the compound every two hours or so on the look out for driver ant columns which appeared with such speed and silence. No one, unless they have seen a driver ant column on the march, can conceive the numbers, the speed, or the ferocity of these insects.

The columns are perhaps two inches wide, and may be two or three miles in length. On the outside walk the soldiers, creatures about half an inch long, with huge heads and great curved jaws. In the middle travel the workers, very much smaller than the soldiers, but still capable of giving a sharp bite. These columns wend their way through the forest, devouring all they come across; if they reach an area which contains a plentiful supply of food they fan out, and within a few minutes the ground is a black, moving carpet of ants. Let one of these columns get into a collection of animals, and within a few minutes your cages would be full of writhing specimens being eaten alive.

My Watchnight was a tall, slim young man, clad in a tiny loin-cloth, and armed with a spear of incredible dimensions. He would arrive at sunset and leave again at dawn. To begin with he was under the impression that I paid him in order that he should get a good night's sleep by the kitchen fire. I quickly put an end to this idea by finding him asleep during his first night's duty, and firing the shotgun off by his ear, with the most gratifying results. He never again slept unless he was sure that I was too tired to wake up and detect him. At first he did not take his duties very seriously; during the day he was employed as a wine tapper and, as all good tappers should, he tasted the wine as he tapped it in order to make sure that it was fit for his customers. Then he would arrive at night, unsteady with the fatigue of this public duty, and fall asleep by the kitchen fire. The shotgun method, when I caught him, never failed to wake him up. But, try as I would, I could not impress him with the danger of ants. His patrol was a half-hearted affair, and only the largest and most widespread attack on the part of the drivers would have come to his notice. Then, one night, he got the fright of his life, and this cured him of his lackadaisical ant-watching.

Every fortnight the village would hold a dance in the centre of the main street. This was a great social event, and everyone would clad themselves in their best print clothes and turn up, to spend the entire night shuffling and swaying in a circle by the flickering light of a small hurricane lamp to the plaintive twittering of one flute, and the solemn thudding of drums. I had been invited to one of these dances and I had gone clad in dressing-gown and pyjamas, armed with a table and chair, the necessary stimulants, and my largest Tilly lamp. The arrival of this monster lamp was greeted with screams of joy by the dancers, for the greatly increased illumination allowed them to see where they were dancing and to perform even more complicated steps. They threw themselves with great zest into the task of entertaining me and when, some two hours later, I went back to bed, I left the Tilly lamp in the midst of the swaying hypnotised circle, with the instructions that it was to be brought back in the morning. This gesture of goodwill had a very good effect and after that, even if work prevented me from going down to the dance myself, I always sent the lamp, and always it was greeted with shouts of joy, handclaps and cries of "Tank you, Masa, tank you . . ." which I could hear even in the camp.

One evening I received a message that the villagers were putting on an extra special dance in my honour and would I, and my lamp, care to take part in the festivities? I said that I was honoured and that, even if I could not manage it, I would be represented by my lamp. It so happened that I finished work earlier than usual, and so I found I could attend. Before going down to the village I gave strict instructions to the Watchnight that, should anything happen in my absence, he was to call me immediately. Then, preceded by the lamp, and followed by my table and chair, I went to join the revels. The dance was good and prolonged. At length I

decided that, if I wanted to get up early the next morning, I
would have to return to bed. Leaving the light to the dancers
I walked back to camp, preceded by a hurricane lamp, and
followed behind by my table and chair. On reaching the
edge of the compound we discovered the Watchnight performing strange antics by the light of his lamp. He was dancing around, occasionally slapping himself and swearing
roundly in Banyangi, and sweeping wildly at the ground with
a small bundle of twigs.

"Watchnight, na whatee?" I called.

"Na ants, sah, na plenty ants."

I rushed across the compound and found the Watchnight
covered with driver ants and the ground a moving carpet. A
steady stream of reinforcements was pouring out of the
bushes. Already the ants were spreading over a wide area,
and some of the advance exploring parties were within a few
feet of the animal house wall. There was no time to be lost
if I wanted to prevent the ants getting in amongst the cages.

"Pious," I yelled, "Augustine, George, Daniel, come
quickly."

They came running across the compound. By this time I
was also covered with ants, and there was nothing for it but
to remove every stitch of clothing. Stark naked I organized
my equally nude staff for battle.

"George, go get dry stick and leaf . . . quick . . . bring
plenty. Pious go get the tins of kerosene. Watchnight and
Daniel, go make the kitchen fire big and bring fire here . . .
quick . . . quick. . . ."

They ran to do what they were told, and I gathered a
handful of leafy twigs and started an attack on the advance
column nearest to the wall of the animal house, sweeping
with all my might with one hand, trying to pluck the biting
ants from my body with the other. George arrived with a
great armful of dry branches and leaves, and these we piled
on top of the main column which was streaming out of the
forest. We soaked the dry sticks with kerosene and set light
to them. Grabbing a tin of kerosene I rushed round and
round the animal house pouring it as I went, while Daniel

ran behind piling sticks on and setting them on fire. Having ringed the animals with fire I felt a bit better, but the fire had to be closely watched to see the sparks from it did not fall on the palm-leaf roof and set the whole house ablaze. It had been a near thing: another few minutes and the vanguard of the ants would have been through the wall and amongst the cages piled in tiers inside. Leaving Pious and George to keep the protecting ring of fire alight, I turned my attention to my tent. To say that it was full of ants means nothing: ants oozed from every part of it, and its green canvas walls were a black moving curtain of ants. Three boxes of skins pinned out to dry were full to overflowing with ants, and the skins were ruined. My bed was being explored very thoroughly by a party of several thousand soldiers, as also were my gun-cases, my clothes box, the traps and nets, and the medicine chest. It took three hours to clear the tent alone; dawn was breaking before we had the invasion under control. We gathered together, naked and dirty, and proceeded to pick the ants from each other's bodies.

My interview with the Watchnight, when I was washed and dressed, and more or less in my right mind, was prolonged and angry. At the end I had him bound and standing between two husky men who were, I informed him, going to take him to the District Office to give him in charge for neglect of duty, attempting to kill me and my collection, sleeping at his post, failing to sound the alarm, and a host of other crimes. I told him, with relish, how the District Officer would take a very stern view of his crimes, and the least he could hope for was two years in jail. At last, cheese-colour with fear, he begged to be let off. With a great show of reluctance I promised him one more chance. But, I warned him, if driver ants came within a hundred yards of the camp again, and he failed to give the alarm, he would be dealt with in the most severe manner. . . . I even hinted darkly at life imprisonment. The threat worked, and after that his night patrols in search of ants were models of perfection, and every driver ant column was seen and headed off in time.

Another thing I had to impress on the Watchnight was

that, should an animal escape from its cage during the night he was directly responsible. Twice animals had found a loose bar, or a corner of wire unnailed, and they had faded into the forest, while the Watchnight snored on his kerosene tin, supporting his nodding head on his enormous spear. Apart from a lecture I did nothing, for the animals in question were common enough and could be procured again. But I determined that, when a suitable opportunity arose, the Watchnight should have a lesson. It happened one evening after dark, that a hunter brought in a half-grown Pangolin. I bought it and placed it in the makeshift box with a variety of things piled on top to prevent its escape. Knowing the strength that these creatures have in their front claws, I warned the Watchnight to keep a close watch on the box to see it did not escape. Before retiring to bed each night I would make a round of all the cages to make sure all was in order, and that every door was securely locked. On peering into the box which had housed the Pangolin I found it empty: how it got out was a mystery, for the articles were still piled undisturbed on top. But I was used to these Houdini-like escapes, and so I did not waste any time trying to puzzle it out. I called to the Watchnight, and pointed to the empty box:

"Watchnight, dis catar beef done run."

"I no see um, sah," mumbled the Watchnight, peering at the box.

"No, I know you no see um, because you no do your job properly. Now, dis beef no get plenty power run quick-quick. Sometime 'e dere dere for bush. Take your light and go look um. If you no find um I go take five shillings from your pay, you hear?"

"I hear, sah," said the Watchnight dismally. He took his lamp and his spear and wandered off into the undergrowth. For an hour I could hear him moving about, breathing heavily, talking to himself to keep his spirits up:

"Catar beef, catar beef, . . . eh . . . aehh! Now, which side dat beef done run? Eh . . . aehh! na trouble too much for me dis ting . . . which side dat blurry beef run? . . . I no see um. . . . Catar beef, you make trouble too much for me. . . ."

At length just as I was dozing off, he uttered a yell of triumph:

"I find um, sah, I done find um here for bush."

"All right, bring um quick."

After some time he reappeared carrying a Pangolin by its tail, beaming delightedly at me. I carried it to the box, noticing as I did so that by lamplight the Pangolin seemed to have grown bigger. Taking the things off the top of the box, I thrust my hand in to shake up the dried banana leaves in the bottom, and my hand touched something round and hard and warm. There, buried under the banana leaves, was the original Pangolin: the Watchnight had caught an entirely different animal! I thrust this new addition inside and went back to bed. It was rather a problem for, by my own laws, the Watchnight should be paid for this new beef he had caught. But to tell him that I had made a mistake, and that the Pangolin had not escaped under his very eyes would, I felt, destroy the lesson. So I decided to say nothing, and salved my conscience by heavily overpaying him for some frogs he brought some days after. He seemed to be an extraordinarily lucky person, for some weeks later he did exactly the same thing with a giant spider that had escaped. This time the spider really had escaped and the Watchnight, hunting for it, discovered another wandering around camp of similar dimension but of a totally different and much rarer species. Bearing his capture back to its box, held gingerly on the end of a stick, he nearly stepped on the original arachnid in the middle of the compound.

These great Palm spiders were one of the few specimens I had that I could never bring myself to like wholeheartedly. Their bodies were the size of an egg and their long legs, spread out, would have exceeded the circumference of a saucer. They were a deep, shiny chocolate in colour, and covered with a thick pelt of tawny fur. Their small glittering eyes seemed to have a nasty evil expression. Most of them, if annoyed or teased with a twig, would retreat, but one or two of them would attack. They could jump two feet in a bound, leaping six inches off the ground or more. They would tilt themselves so that their great curved fangs could come into play, and the first pair of legs would be outspread, welcoming you into their hairy embrace. That their bite was poisonous I knew, but I doubt if it could kill you unless you were prone to blood poisoning.

One afternoon a man turned up with two little wicker baskets, one containing a fat, beautiful, and deadly Gaboon viper, and the other one of these revolting Palm spiders. When I had purchased them, the man asked me if I could attend to his hand which was wrapped up in a filthy piece of cloth. He had a deep wound in the thumb, which was slightly discoloured and swollen. I examined it, washed it, and put a clean bandage on. Then I asked him what had caused the wound.

"Beef done chop me," he said laconically, gesturing at the baskets.

"Good God," I said, really startled, "which beef, the snake or the other?"

"Oh, no, sah, not de snake . . . dat other beef . . . it de pain me too much, Masa. You no fit give me some kind of medicine for dis bite, sah?"

I gave him two aspirins and a strong glass of vivid yellow lime-juice, and assured him that it would cure him. He was very gratified, and returned the next day to ask for some more of that medicine that had done his bite so much good. I offered him two more aspirins, but he refused them. No, he didn't want that medicine, he wanted the yellow one, as that was the one that had really done the trick.

Another aspect of the Cameroon mentality was demonstrated to me one day when a small boy appeared carrying a tortoise. On examination it proved to have a large hole bored in its shell, thus ruining it as a specimen, so I gave it back to the child and told him I did not want it, and why. Half an hour later another child appeared carrying the same tortoise. Thinking perhaps the first child's tender years had prevented him from understanding, I explained all over again. Shortly afterwards a bigger child arrived carrying the same reptile. During the course of the day different people, ranging from toddlers to old men, all appeared and offered for sale the same wretched tortoise.

"Why," I asked the last man who brought it, "why all you different people bring the same same beef eh? I done tell all dis different man dat I no go buy dis beef . . . look . . . 'e get hole for his back, you no see? Why you bring um so many times?"

"Eh, sometime if Masa no go buy from me he go buy from other man," answered the tortoise's temporary owner.

"Listen, my friend, you go tell your family that I no want dis beef, you hear? And if any man bring this beef to me again, I go beat him until he get hole for larse same same dis beef, understand?"

"Yes, sah," he said, smiling, "Masa no want."

And that was the last I saw of the tortoise.

Another peculiar attitude of mind on the part of the beef bringers was the firm belief that, no matter how mangled a specimen was, I could be persuaded to buy it, by the simple process of telling me it was not hurt, and would, in all probability, live for years. This applied particularly to birds. At first, the brigade of small boys who tapped the forest creepers to obtain the white rubber-like substance which was used as bird-lime, were firmly convinced that all I wanted was a bird. As long as it was still breathing, it mattered not that most of its feathers were missing, or if it had broken a leg or two. It took some time, and some pretty stiff arguments, to persuade them otherwise. The thing that really convinced them was the episode of the Pygmy Rails.

One morning I was examining the usual collection of wicker fish-traps crammed full of maimed birds which the boys had brought, and delivering a lecture on careful treatment of specimens. Just as I was unleashing my scorn and annoyance on this shuffling collection of teen-age beef bringers and their dreadful collection of birds, a small girl, perhaps six years old, wandered into the compound carrying a small receptacle cleverly woven out of dry grass and leaves. She came to a halt in front of me and, after surveying me silently and appraisingly for a moment, held out her basket.

"Na whatee?" I inquired.

"Na bird, Masa," she piped.

I took the basket from her hands and peered into it, resigning myself to the fact that here was yet another basket full of useless creatures. Inside crouched three beautiful little birds, unhurt, and without a feather out of place. They had slender legs, and long delicate toes which, in the hands

White-spotted Pygmy Rail

of normal bird trappers, would most certainly have been broken. No feathers had been pulled out of the wings, a favourite method of preventing a specimen flying away. They were in perfect condition. This, I felt, was too good an opportunity to miss. Picking out one of the Pygmy Rails I showed it silently to the gaping boys.

"Look," I said, "here na picken woman who savvay catch bird pass you man picken. Look dis bird: he no get wound, he no get rope for his legs. Dis kind of bird I go buy, he no go die. If dis woman picken fit catch bird why you men picken no fit, eh? Now, you go see how much I go give for dis bird."

Turning to the girl I asked her how much she wanted for her specimens.

"Two two shillings, Masa," she replied, meaning two shillings each.

"You hear?" I asked the boys. "Dis picken say she want

two two shilling for dis bird. Na fine price dat: she get good bird, she done catch um softly softly, he no get wound, and she no bring um with rope for 'e foot. Because she savvay catch beef pass you all I go pay her five five shillings for dis very good beef."

"Eh . . . aehh!" groaned the boys in envy and astonishment. The girl, who had not understood what was being said, was so amazed that I should pay her more than twice what she had asked, that she clutched the money to her chest and fled the compound as fast as her fat little legs could carry her, in case I should change my mind. The boys followed in a chattering gesticulating group. From that day onwards the birds brought in were excellent, with one or two exceptions, and the boys of the village waxed fat on the proceeds of their sales, and my cages started to fill with some lovely specimens.

The boys had two methods of catching birds and, although both were effective, the best was the use of what was known as "lubber". In the forest grew a certain vine and, on being cut, this yielded a copious flow of thick white sap. The boys would collect this as it ran, as fast as blood, from the wounded vine, and when they had collected about half a cupful they would place it over a slow fire, having first mixed in the juice of a curious red fruit which tasted exactly like lemon. After boiling for a couple of hours this brew would be set aside to cool, and left overnight. In the morning it would be like a thick, resilient paste, extraordinarily sticky. Then the trappers would get the long slender midribs from a palm tree and coat them with this mixture. Going to certain small forest pools at which they knew the birds would congregate, they would then stick groups of these ribs in the sand in a fan shape. For some curious reason the birds, on coming down to drink, would rather perch on these twigs than on the sand. Landing on one the bird would find that its feet were held fast, and in its fluttering to get free it would fall forwards or backwards on to the other twigs, which would then stick all over its plumage, rendering it helpless. After a few hours this bird-lime dried on the feathers, and the birds would clean it off themselves by normal preening methods. It was by far the most satisfactory method of catching birds I have seen, apart from netting them.

The second method employed was the use of a curious and rather ingenious trap. A springy stick was curved like a bow, and tied. From the base of the stick, cleverly balanced, was a small perch, and when it was in position it kept the bow bent at the ready. On the end of this little perch was placed a bait, and over the perch was draped a fine noose, which was attached to the main bow string. When the bird settled on the twig to get the bait, its weight would knock the perch down, which would release the bow, which, in turn, would pull the noose tight around the bird's legs. This, as I say, was a very effective method, but the trouble was that if the strength of your bow was too great it would pull the noose tight, and probably break both the bird's legs. Also, if it did not do this, the bird would be hanging there by its legs, and unless removed from the trap quickly, would maim its own legs by fluttering. Of the two I found the bird-lime the best, and after a time refused to buy birds that had been caught by the other method. With bird-lime they seemed to catch everything: the scarlet and black Malimbus, with their steel-blue, finch-like beaks; the Robin Chats with their white eyebrow stripes and their wings marked with an azure blue patch, like a jay; the Forest Robins, almost identical with the English robin in size and colour, except that their backs were a deeper brown, their breasts a richer, redder orange, and with a small white spot on their cheeks, just near the corner of their beaks. The Blue-spotted Doves, neat grey and fawn birds with their wings spotted with glittering feathers of green, and many other kinds of dove and pigeon were caught, also the brilliant Pygmy Kingfishers, and the Shining-blue Kingfisher, and an endless array of Weaver birds.

CHAPTER SEVEN

Drills, Dances and Drums

To supply all the insectivorous birds with sufficient live food was a great problem, and I overcame it in this way. I employed a gang of perhaps twenty young children, armed them with bottles, and sent them out to hunt grasshoppers. They were paid by the results, not for the time they spent. A penny for thirty insects was the usual price. Another band of children was employed to go into the forest and collect the curious termite nests shaped like gigantic mushrooms, that grew in the gloomy places. These nests, constructed out of hard brown mud, were split open on a canvas sheet, and from the honeycomb of tunnels and passages inside would pour thousands of tiny termites and their fat white young. It was these soft plump youngsters that the birds relished. These nests could be stored for about twenty-four hours before the termites, under cover of darkness (for they shun the light) would vacate them, so in the corner of the animal house there was always a pile of fresh termite nests on hand for feeding, and all through the day a stream of fat-bellied toddlers would arrive at the camp, carrying on their heads these mushroom-like objects. A line of these children wending their way through the forest towards the camp, the mushrooms perched on their woolly heads, laughing and chattering in shrill little voices, had a peculiar, gnome-like quality about them.

These termite hunters often found different creatures while they were in the forest, and these specimens were then brought in triumph when they appeared with the nests. The commonest thing they came across were the chameleons, which they were quite convinced were deadly poisonous, and they would carry them fearfully on the extreme end of a long stick, screaming loudly if the reptile made any sort of movement in their direction. The most common chameleon they found was the Flap-necked species, a beast about eight inches long, generally a bright leaf-green in colour. This species was full of fight, and when caught they would turn from bright green to dirty grey, covered with evil brown blotches. Opening their mouths wide they would sway from side to side, hissing loudly. If picked up when they were like this they would turn without hesitation and give you quite a sharp bite, though not sufficient to draw blood. Hissing and swaying, their bulging eyes revolving madly in an effort to see all ways at once, these miniature prehistoric monsters would be borne into camp, clasping the end of the stick desperately with their parrot-like feet.

It was the termite hunters that brought me my first Horned chameleon, a creature so fantastic that at first I could hardly believe my eyes. It was smaller than the Flap-necked, and of a more slender build. It lacked the great helmet on its head, ornamented with the bright blue beads of skin, that the Flap-necked could boast, and its colours were quieter and more sedate. But its face was incredible: from the nose there grew two horns, sharply pointed, slightly curved, and about half an inch long. They looked exactly like the curving tusks of a miniature elephant. On the top of its nose, slightly behind, and midway between these two tusks, grew another. This was longer than the others, and quite straight, rather the type of thing a unicorn was supposed to have. From behind this barricade of tusks the prominent eyes would revolve with a fishy and extraordinarily intelligent expression. The body colour of this creature was a nice pearl-grey, heavily patterned with light brown marks. When angry or annoyed it would turn a deep, almost black, maroon colour, marbled with patches of bright rust red, like big fingerprints. I presumed that these horns on its nose were used for defence and perhaps for mating battles, so when I had some time to spare I performed a series of experiments with this specimen. First I picked him up and, though he tried to bite, he did not use his horns to butt my hand with, as I had expected. Thinking that he was not sufficiently annoyed I placed him on the ground and teased him with a twig. Although he changed colour, hissed, and even snapped at the twig, he made no attempt to use his horns. Some time after another Horned chameleon was brought in, and then I set out to discover if the horns were reserved exclusively for battles with members of the same species. I placed both chameleons on a long branch, facing each other and about three feet apart. At first they both merely sat there and let their natural colour ebb back after the shock of this sudden change. When their normal colour was more or less restored, they proceeded to crawl towards one another, and I waited eagerly for the battle. When they came face to face there was no room for them to pass on the narrow branch, so one simply walked over the other's back in that completely impersonal way that reptiles have. Slightly annoyed, I replaced them in their former positions, but once again they proceeded to crawl over each other, each completely ignoring the other's presence. So there it was: I was no nearer to discovering the use of the horns than I had been before. During all the time I kept these reptiles I never saw them make a movement that could be interpreted as a use of the horns, either in defence or in battle.

I had always considered chameleons easy things to keep but I discovered that they could be just as temperamental as a monkey or a duiker if they wanted to be. In a cage they did not seem to get enough air or sunlight. Once I placed three of them in a rather exposed position and they all promptly died of sunstroke. At last, after much experiment, I found the best way to treat them. On four saplings in the corner of the compound I had a palm-leaf roof erected, and under this, tethered by the waist with fine grass cords to branches, I kept my chameleons. They were tied about three feet apart, so they would not crawl over each other and get their ropes entangled, and in front of each one was suspended a lump of rotting meat. This attracted the flies in hundreds and the chameleons would squat there, rolling their eyes, and flipping their six-inch tongues out, and every time they would hit a fly amidships. Three times a day they had to be sprayed with water, which they did not seem to enjoy very much, but without this treatment they sickened and died.

There was a third species of chameleon in the Cameroons, and my first meeting with this rare reptile was unusual to say the least. One afternoon I had decided to attack several large termites' nests which dotted the fields and low undergrowth which lay outside the village and within easy reach of the camp. I had gathered about twenty people to help me, as a large area around the nests had to be closed in with nets, and you needed plenty of people to patrol these and remove anything that was caught. Arriving at the first nest, a massive red earth fortress some twelve feet high and about thirty feet around the base, we commenced to clear away all the surrounding undergrowth and leave an open space round the nest. When this was done the usual selection of mysterious holes was brought to light. Round the edge of this clearing we had made, we strung the nets, and posted the excited helpers at intervals along them. Then we blocked up most of the holes in the nest and, lighting a bundle of dry grass, thrust it down a hole and stood back. Slowly the smoke drifted along the tunnels and appeared at the mouths of other holes, little coiling skeins at first which rapidly turned into great rolling clouds as more and more fuel was added. We all waited in a tense silence as we watched the smoke. A quarter of an hour passed, and not a sign of life came from the nests. I had just decided that it must be devoid of life when a great uproar started at the other side of the hill. Hurrying round I found Elias and Carpenter convulsed with laughter. Choking with mirth they pointed into the smoke, and peering I could see, at the mouth of the largest hole, a tiny chameleon, about three inches long, staggering out into the fresh air.

"Masa, we done catch big beef to-day," roared Elias, slapping his plump thighs in an excess of mirth.

DRILLS, DANCES, AND DRUMS

I picked the chameleon up and placed him in the palm of my hand. He was, as I say, no more than three inches long, and had a tiny stumpy little tail about an inch and a half long, which was curled up neatly like a watch-spring. On the end of his upturned nose was a small horn, which gave him a very disdainful, camel-like expression. He was a light fawn, covered with faint specks and streaks of rust red. He was my first Pygmy chameleon, and I was fascinated by his size, by his unhurried movements, and by his disdainful expression. Why he, an essentially arboreal reptile, should be found in the tunnels of a termites' nest I could not think, but there he was. Later, when I got to know him better, I discovered other curious things about him. I never saw him eat, for example, yet he must have done so, for he stayed with me a long time and remained plump and in the best of health. I could not get him to change colour at all, either by annoying him, or by putting him on different coloured surroundings. The only time he changed was at night, when he would close his eyes and turn a delicate ash grey all over, thus looking more like a small dead leaf than ever. I eventually obtained four of these amusing little creatures, but I was never lucky enough to see one in its wild state, except the one in the termites' nest, which I don't think counts! Each time, when they were brought to me, I would ask the bringer where it had been caught, and each time they would say that they had captured it on the ground, generally walking solemnly along a native path. With the other chameleons they always insisted that they caught them in the trees, but the Pygmys they found on the ground. Careful questioning failed to shake them on this point. Wondering if perhaps these little reptiles were quite so exclusively arboreal as I had supposed, I made an experiment with the four I had. I placed them in a cage which had, in addition to numerous branches, a layer of earth at the bottom covered with dead leaves and bits of twigs. Hitherto they had been forced to remain in the branches because of the bareness of the cage bottom. As soon as some natural cover was available down below, they left the branches and lived entirely on the ground, hiding happily among the leaves.

The only habit they had which was exactly like their larger cousins, was the dance. This is a most curious action which chameleons indulge in occasionally, and which really has to be seen to be appreciated to the full. Place them on the ground, or on a branch, and they will stand stock still for a minute or so, only their eyes moving. Then, very slowly, they will put forward one front leg and the opposite hind leg. With these two members in mid-air they will sway rhythmically backwards and forwards for a few seconds. Then they will take the step and stand stock still again before repeating the performance with the other pair of legs. All the time their great eyes would be rolling round and round, looking up and down, back and front.

Neither the Africans nor my collection of monkeys appreciated the chameleons. The Africans would have nothing to do with them, alive or dead, and the sight of my handling and being bitten by these reptiles would set them all off moaning and clicking their fingers in agitation. They considered that every chameleon was deadly poisonous, and no argument would convince them otherwise. The monkeys made it quite obvious that they disliked and feared these reptiles, but not in the same way as they feared a snake. The chameleons fascinated them and revolted them at the same time. The monkeys were tethered to stakes next door to the shelter that housed the chameleons, and they never tired of watching the reptiles moving slowly about their branches. Whenever a chameleon would shoot out his tongue for a fly, all the monkeys would start back as though bitten, and utter sharp cries of wonder and interest.

At this time my monkey collection consisted of a Red-eared Guenon, four Putty-nose Guenons, and six Drills, and one day I tried an experiment. One of the chameleons had died, and so I took the corpse to the monkeys, and sitting down among them I showed it to them. They formed a respectful circle round me and examined the chameleon with interest. After screwing up his courage the eldest Drill touched it quickly, then drew back his hand and wiped it hastily on the ground. I could not persuade the Guenons to come anywhere near it. The Drills eventually became very brave and started to play with the corpse, even chasing the screaming Guenons with it and threatening them. I had to put a stop to this as the Drills were quite bad-mannered enough, and the Guenons were protesting bitterly, and seemed genuinely terrified. Then I tried something else: I got a large live chameleon and let it walk amongst the monkeys. Although they kept out of its way and chattered and made faces at it, they did not seem more than slightly afraid. I then got a fair-sized water-snake and released that. There was no mistaking the fear this time: they all fled to the top of their stakes and clung there screaming blue murder until I had removed the snake.

Drill

The Drills were the street urchins of the monkey collection. Everything, or almost everything, that you gave to them was first put through the test of whether it was edible or not. If it was not, then it was played with for a while, but they soon lost interest. If a thing was edible (and few things did not come into this category) they would treat it in two different ways. If it was a delicacy, such as a grasshopper, they would cram it into their mouths with all speed in order to prevent anyone else having it. If it was something that was not *very* attractive they would play with it for a long time, occasionally taking bites out of it, until there was nothing left for them to play with. The Drills, though ugly in comparison to some monkeys, had a brand of charm all their own. Their rolling, dog-like walk; the way they would wrinkle up their noses at you, showing all their baby teeth in a hideous grimace which was supposed to be ingratiating; the way they would walk backwards towards you, displaying their bright pink bottoms as a sign of affection. All these things endeared the Drills to me, but the thing that never failed to melt my heart was the trustful way they would rush to your legs as soon as you appeared, and cling there with hands and feet, uttering hiccuping cries of delight, and peering up into your face with such trustful expressions.

The six Drills I had acquired ruled the roost over all the other and more timid monkeys for a long time. The slender and nervous Guenons could always be persuaded to drop a succulent grasshopper if a Drill charged them, uttering guttural coughs of anger. But one day a new arrival proved their reign at an end: a man walked into the camp, preceded on a length of rope by a three parts grown Baboon. Young though he was, he was at least three times as big as the largest drill, and so, from the moment I purchased him, he assumed control of the monkeys. Apart from his great size he had a shaggy coat of yellowish fur, huge teeth, and a long sweeping, lion-like tail. It was this latter that seemed to give the Drills an inferiority complex: they would examine it for a long time with intense interest, and then turn round and gaze at their own blunt posteriors, ornamented only with a short curled stump of a tail. I called this baboon George, for he resembled a character in the village with this name, and he turned out to be gentle and kind to the other monkeys, without allowing them to take any liberties. Sometimes he would go so far as to allow the Guenons to search for salt on his skin, while he lay prostrate on the ground, a trance-like expression on his face. When he first arrived the Drills banded together and tried to give him a beating up, to prove their superiority, but George was equal to the occasion and gave far more than he got. After this the Drills were very respectful indeed, and would even give a quick look round to see where George was before bullying a Guenon, for George's idea of settling a quarrel was to rush in and bite both contestants as hard as he could.

George, owing to the fact that he was so tame, was a great favourite with the staff, and spent much of his time in the kitchen. This, however, I had to put a stop to as he was used as an excuse for almost anything that happened: if dinner was late, George had upset the frying-pan; if something was missed there were always at least three witnesses to the fact that George had been seen with it last. So in the end George was tethered among the other monkeys and accepted the leadership without letting it go to his head. In this respect he was most unusual, for almost any monkey, if he sees that all the others respect and are afraid of him, will turn into the most disgusting bully. He also did something that astonished not only his fellow-monkeys, but the staff as well. Thinking that he would show the same respect for the chameleons as the other monkeys did, I tied him with a fairly long leash, and his first action was to walk to the full extent of it, reach out a black paw, snatch a chameleon off its branch, and proceed to eat it with every sign of enjoyment. I hastily shortened his leash.

The Red-eared Guenon was the most delightful of the monkeys. About the size of a small cat, she was a delicate green-yellow colour on her body, with yellow patches on her cheeks, a fringe of russet hair hiding her ears, and on her nose a large heart-shaped patch of red hair. Her limbs were slender, and she had great thin bony fingers, like a very old man's. Every day the monkeys had a handful of grasshoppers each, and the Red-eared Guenon, when she saw me coming, would stand up on her hind legs, uttering shrill bird-like twitterings, and holding out her long arms beseechingly, her thin fingers trembling. She would fill her mouth and both hands with grasshoppers, and when the last insect had been scrunched she would carefully examine the front and back of her hands to make sure she had not missed one, and then would search the ground all round, an intense expression in her light brown eyes. She was the most gentle monkey I had ever come across, and even her cries were this delicate bird-like twittering, and a long drawn-out "wheeeee-eep" when she was trying to attract one's attention, so different from the belching grunts and loud, unruly screams of the Drills, or the tinny screech of the Putty-noses. George seemed to share my liking for this Guenon, and she seemed to find comfort in being near to his massive body. Peering from behind his shaggy shoulders she would even pluck up the courage to make faces at the Drills.

At midday the sun beat down upon the forest and the camp, and all the birds fell silent in the intense sticky heat. The only sound was the faint, far-away whisper of the cicadas in the cool depths of the forest. The birds drowsed in their cages with their eyes closed, the rats lay on their back sound asleep, their little paws twitching. Under their palm-leaf shelter the monkeys would be stretched out full length on the warm ground, blissfully dreaming, angelic expressions on their little faces. The only one who rarely had an afternoon siesta was the Red-eared Guenon: she would squat by George's recumbent, heavily breathing form, industriously cleaning his fur, uttering soft little cries of encouragement to herself, as absorbed as an old woman at a spinning-wheel. With her long fingers she would part the hair, peering at the pink skin beneath, in this exciting search. She was not searching for fleas: it cannot be said too often that no monkey searches another for fleas. Should they happen upon a flea, which would be unusual, during the search, it would, of course, be eaten. No, the real reason that monkeys search each other's fur is to obtain the tiny flakes of salt which appear after the sweat has evaporated from the skin: these flakes of salt are a great delicacy in the monkey world. The searcher is rewarded by this titbit, while the one who is searched is compensated by the delightful tickly sensation he receives, as his fur is ruffled and parted by the other's fingers. Sometimes the position would be reversed and the

Guenon would lie on the ground with her eyes closed in ecstasy while George searched her soft fur with his big, black, clumsy fingers. Sometimes he would get so absorbed that he would forget he was not dealing with a monkey his own size, and he would handle her a trifle roughly. The only protest she would make would be her soft twittering cry, and then George would realize what he had done and grunt apologetically.

At night the monkeys were untied from their stakes, given a drink of milk with cod liver oil in it, and then tied up inside a special small hut I had built for them, next door to my tent. The nearer they were to me at night the safer I felt, for I never knew when a local leopard might fancy monkey for his nightly feed, and tied out in the middle of the compound they would not stand a chance. So, each night the monkeys would be carried to their house, dripping milk, and screaming because they did not want to go to bed. George was last, and while the others were being tethered he would make a hasty round of all the pots, hoping against hope that one of the others had left a drop of milk. Then he too, protesting strongly, would be dragged off to bed. One night George revolted. After they had all been put to bed, and I had had my supper, I went down to a dance in the village. George must have watched me going through a crack in his bedroom wall, and he decided that if I could spend an evening out he could also. Very carefully he unpicked his tether and quietly eased his way through the palm-leaf wall. Then he slipped across the compound, and was just gaining the path when the Watchnight saw him.

The Watchnight uttered a wild cry, seized a banana and rushed forward to try and tempt him back. George paused and watched his approach. He let him get within a foot or so of his trailing leash, then he ran forward, bit the poor man in the calf of the leg, and fled down the path towards the village, leaving the Watchnight standing on one leg and screaming. On reaching the village George was surprised to see so many people gathered round a Tilly lamp. Just as he arrived the "band" struck up, and the crowd broke into the shuffling, swaying dance that was the favourite Eshobi at that time. George watched them for a moment, astonished, and then decided that this was a very superior game which had been arranged for his special benefit. Uttering a loud scream he rushed into the circle of dancers, his trailing rope tripping several couples up, and then he proceeded to leap and scream in the centre of the circle, occasionally making a rush at a passing dancer. Then he overturned the Tilly lamp which promptly went out. Scared of the dark and the pandemonium his sudden appearance had caused, he rushed to the nearest person and clung to his legs, screaming with all his might.

Eventually the lamp was relit, George was chastised and seated on my knee, where he behaved very well, taking sips out of my glass when I wasn't looking, and watching the dancers with an absorbed expression. The dancers, keeping a wary eye on him, once more formed a circle. Presently I called for a small drum and, putting George on the ground, I gave the instrument to him. He had been watching the band with great attention and knew just what to do. He squatted there showing his great canines in a huge grin of delight, beating the drum with all his might. Unfortunately his sense of rhythm was not as good as the other drummers and his erratic playing threw the dancers into confusion once again, so I was forced to take the drum away from him and send him off to bed, protesting loudly all the way.

George attended one other dance, and this was by special request. Two days before I left Eshobi to go and join John at Bakebe, the chief arrived to say that the village was throwing a dance as a sort of farewell party for me. They would be very glad if I would attend, and could I bring the monkey that played the drum as a friend of the chief's was coming to the dance and he was very anxious to see this feat performed by a monkey. I promised that both George and I would be there. The Tilly lamps were polished and lit, and both transported down to the village half an hour before my arrival. When I arrived, clad in my dressing-gown and pyjamas, George walking sedately beside me on his leash, we were greeted with much handclapping and cries of "welcome". I was surprised to see such a large crowd, all dressed in their very best clothes, which ranged from a boy clad in a very fetching two-piece costume made out of old flour sacks with the name of the brand printed in large blue letters across his posterior, to the council and chief who were dressed in their brightest ceremonial robes. Elias I hardly recognized: he was to be the Master of Ceremonies, and had dressed himself to kill; plimsoles on his great feet, a bright green shirt, and brown pin-striped trousers. He had an enormous watch-chain on the end of which was a huge whistle which he kept blowing frantically to restore order. The band was the largest yet: three drums, two flutes, and a triangle.

As soon as my table and chair had been set up, and I had shaken hands with the council members and the chief, and exchanged a few complimentary words, Elias sallied into the middle of the street, and stood between the Tilly lamps blowing the whistle for silence. Then he spoke:

"All you people savvay na dis last dance we get Masa. So all you people go dance fine, show Masa what kind of fine dance we make for Eshobi, you hear?"

A roar of delight came from the crowd, and they surged forward to form a circle. Elias stood in the centre of the circle, signalled the band, and they were off. Elias danced round and round inside of the circle, wagging his bottom and roaring instructions to the dancers:

"*Advance* . . . meet and waltz . . . right turn . . . let we set . . . *all* move . . . back we set again. . . . *Advance* . . . right turn . . . meet and waltz . . . conduct for yourself . . . back we set. . . . *Advance* . . ." and so on. The dancers bobbed and shuffled round to his directions, arms, legs, bodies, eyes, all dancing, their shadows thrown large and grotesque by the lamps, sliding and interweaving on the red earth. The drums thumped and stuttered in a complicated rhythm, and the flutes bound it together with their thin cries. On and on went the dance, faster and faster, the dancers' faces gleaming in the lamplight, their eyes glazed, their bodies twisting and their feet stamping until the earth shook. The watchers

clapped and swayed, and occasionally ejaculated an appreciative "eh . . . aehh!" as some young blood executed a particularly complicated step. At length, through sheer exhaus-
tion, the band stopped and the dance was at an end. Everyone
sat down and the buzz of conversation filled the air.

Presently, after three or four more dances, Elias approached leading a detestable youth called Samuel by the
hand. Samuel was a most objectionable young man, a product of a Mission School education which made him speak
in that stilted style of English which I detested. However,
he was the only one in the village that could speak proper
English, Elias explained, and he was to act as interpreter,
for the chief council member was about to make a speech.
The chief council member rose to his feet on the other side
of the street, drew his lovely pale pink robes closer about
him, and commenced to speak loudly, volubly, and rapidly
in Banyangi. Samuel had taken a place by his side and listened carefully. At the end of each sentence he would rush
across the treet, translate into English for me, and then rush
back to catch the next sentence. At first the council member
would wait for Samuel to return before starting the next sentence, but as the speech progressed he got carried away by
his own flow of words, and poor Samuel was kept dashing
to and fro at some speed. The night was warm and Samuel
unused to such exercise; his white shirt was soon grey with
sweat. The speech, as translated to me, went something like
this:

"People of Eshobi! You all know why we are here to-
night . . . to say good-bye to the master who has been with
us for so long. Never in the whole history of Eshobi have
we had such a master . . . money has flowed as freely from
him as water in the river-bed. (As it was a dry season and
most of the rivers a mere trickle, I felt this was hardly complimentary.) Those who had the power went to bush and
caught beef, for which they were paid handsomely. Those
who were weak, the women and children, could obtain salt
and money by bringing grasshoppers and white ants. We,
the elders of the village, would like the master to settle down

here: we would give him land, and build him a fine house.
But he must go back to his own country with the beef that
we of Eshobi have got for him. We can only hope that he
tells the people of his country how we of Eshobi tried to
help him, and to hope that, on his next tour, he will come
back here and stay even longer."

This speech was followed by prolonged cheers, under
cover of which Samuel was helped away by a friend. I then
rose and thanked them for their kindness, and promised that
I would come back if I could, for I had grown very fond of
Eshobi and all the inhabitants. This, indeed, was quite true.
I spoke in my very best pidgin, and apologized for not being
able to speak in their own language. Tumultuous cheers followed, aided and abetted by George, who yelled his applause
loudly. Then the band struck up again, George was given a
drum and proceeded to play it with great dash and vigour to
the amazement and delight of the visiting tribesman. It was
very late when I led George, yawning prodigiously on the
end of his leash, back to the camp. The dance went on until
dawn flamed in the sky.

We worked all night before we left, packing up the animals, tying the cages into suitable head-loads. At five
o'clock the entire village turned out: half were to act as
carriers for my large collection, and the other half had come
to see me off. The cook had been sent on ahead to prepare
breakfast at Mamfe, where we were to be picked up by the
lorry. Slowly the camp site disintegrated. Loads were carefully tested, all the more valuable specimens being given to
the most trustworthy carriers. The women carried the palm
mats, the collecting equipment, the kitchen things, and other
items of little value, and they were sent on ahead. Then the
carriers with the animals picked up their loads and followed.
I disposed of a pile of empty tins and bottles to various hunters and others in the village who had come to say good-bye,
as these things were most valuable in their eyes. Then, accompanied by a dense crowd of villagers all rushing to shake
my hand and say good-bye, I walked to the banks of the
small stream outside the village, where the forest path began.

ESHOBI

More handshaking, white teeth gleaming, cries of good-bye, and I crossed the stream and started in pursuit of the carriers, whose voices I could hear echoing in the depths of the forest ahead.

By the time my long line of carriers had emerged from the forest into the grass fields, dawn had broken. The sky was azure blue, and the rising sun was gilding the tops of the forest trees. Ahead of us, across the grass field and the line of carriers, three hornbills flew, honking wildly and soulfully as hornbills will. Elias turned to me, his face gleaming with sweat, a great cage of fruit bats balanced on his head.

"Dis bird sorry too much, sah, that you leave Eshobi," he said.

I, also, was sorry too much that I was leaving Eshobi.

Part Two

BAKEBE, AND BEYOND

CHAPTER EIGHT

Snakes and Sunbirds

At Bakebe I found that John had obtained permission to live in a huge native hut that had once done duty as a Public Works Department store. It was a three-sided structure, light and airy, perched on top of a hill above the village. This vantage-point gave us a magnificent view over an endless, undulating sea of forest, to the French Cameroon borders and beyond. Every conceivable shade of green seemed to have been used in the composition of this picture, with here and there a bombax tree glowing like a great bonfire, its branches full of scarlet flowers and sunbirds. There were feathery, delicate trees in pale green; thick-set oak-like trees with deep olive leaves; tall, spreading, aristocratic trees, whose pale silver trunks stretched up elegantly several hundred feet from the ground, and whose slender branches negligently supported a mass of shimmering yellow-green leaves, as well as the deep green, untidy bundles of orchids and tree ferns that clung to its bark. Curious hills rose from the forest on all sides, hills shaped as perfect isosceles triangles, as square as bricks, or ridged and humped as the back of an old crocodile, and each one covered to its summit with the shaggy cloak of forest. In the early morning, looking out from under our hill-top, the forest would be invisible under the blanket of white mist; as the sun rose this dispersed, twisting and coiling in great columns up to the blue sky, so that it seemed as though the whole forest was on fire. Soon the mist would only cling round the curiously shaped hills, so that they looked like islands in a sea of milk.

Bakebe, I soon found, was a good place for reptiles. Half a mile away was a deep broad river, and every so often a small boy would appear with a baby Broad-fronted Crocodile dangling from a noose of grass. On arrival I had had a pool constructed for the crocodiles, and I found very soon that I was forced to enlarge it. Every week I had a count of the inmates of the pool, as I had a shrewd suspicion that unless I did this I might be buying the same reptiles over and over again. These counts were exciting affairs which generally ended in the animal staff having bandaged fingers. It is astonishing how hard even a six-inch crocodile can bite when it puts its mind to it. Needless to say the staff did not look upon this duty with any enthusiasm: they considered it a most dangerous occupation, and always tried to shirk it if they could.

One day the staff had been more dilatory than usual over their duties and so, more as a punishment than anything, I told them to go and count the crocodiles. Presently I heard a loud wail, followed by a crashing sound and a splash. Hurrying out I found chaos reigning at the pool: Daniel, in climbing the fence, had slipped and fallen against it, and the entire side, not having been designed to withstand this sort of treatment, had given way. Daniel had then completed the destruction by rolling into the pool, and thus scaring some forty baby surians out of the water, up on to the bank, and so out of the broken fence. When I arrived the ground was covered with crocodiles. They scuttled in all directions with great speed and agility, their mouths open threateningly. The Africans, who were unshod, were also moving with speed and agility. I yelled for reinforcements, and the household staff rushed from the kitchen to join in the chase, and they were followed by the bird staff from the house. In times of crisis such as this, everyone, no matter what his station or job, was called upon to lend a hand. Well in the rear, upholding the Englishman's traditional reputation for calmness, came John, in his normal slow and unhurried manner.

By the time he arrived on the scene most of the reptiles had taken cover in the surrounding undergrowth. Peering round he could only see one or two crocodiles in sight, and so naturally wanted to know what all the shouting and fuss was for.

"I thought *all* the crocs had escaped," he said aggrievedly. "That's why I came down."

As if in answer, five crocodiles appeared out of the grass and converged about his feet. John looked at them broodingly for a minute, unaffected by the cries of alarm from the bird staff, and then he bent down and, picking one carefully up by the tail, he waved it at me.

"Here's one, old boy," he called.

"Don't hold it like that, John," I called, "it will turn . . ."

Acting as if under instructions the tiny reptile curved itself up and fastened its jaws on John's finger. To his credit let it be said that not a sound escaped him; he shook the reptile free, not without some effort, and backed away from the battle area.

"I don't think I will join in after all, if you don't mind," he said, sucking his fingers, "I am *supposed* to be a *bird* man." He retired to the hut and fastened an enormous bandage round his finger, while the rest of us spent a hot and painful hour rounding up the remaining crocodiles, and mending the fence.

This incident was the beginning of a whole row of irritating episodes in John's life, all of which involved reptiles. He insisted that all these episodes took place at my instigation: before my return from Eshobi, he said, he had led a happy and reptile-free existence. As soon as I appeared on the scene the reptile world, so to speak, converged on him. John was not afraid of snakes, but he treated them with caution and respect and, while able to appreciate their beauty from afar, he did not want them on too intimate a footing with him. And so the fact that, for a short time, reptiles in general and snakes in particular seemed to find him irresistible, was a source of considerable annoyance to him. Not long after the escape of the crocodiles John's finger was healing nicely, and the second episode occurred.

I was just leaving the hut one day to go and examine some traps I had set, when a man arrived with a wicker fish-trap full of water-snakes. Now these snakes, I was fairly sure, were non-poisonous. Even if venomous they would only be mildly so. As I was in a hurry I purchased the creatures and pushed them into an empty kerosene tin and placed a plank on top, meaning to attend to them on my return. When I got back that evening I found that the carpenter had removed the plank to convert it into a cage, and all the water-snakes had disappeared. As this had happened in the open I presumed that the reptiles had dashed back to the forest so, beyond lecturing the carpenter on carelessness, I did nothing. Half an hour later John was doing some moving in the bird section, and on lifting up a large and heavy cage was startled to find five fat water-snakes coiled up beneath it. Unfortunately, in his surprise, he let fall one end of the cage, which landed on his instep. There followed a hectic chase, during which John had to move most of his bird-cages as the reptiles slid from one to the other with great rapidity. John was not amused, and his short soliloquy on the reptile kingdom (in which he included me) was a joy to listen to.

A few days later a panting boy rushed up from the village and informed me that there was a snake in a banana tree, and would I go and catch it. It so happened that the entire staff was out on various errands, and so John was the only one to whom I could appeal for help. Very reluctantly he left his bird feeding and accompanied me down the hill-side. At the village we found a crowd of about fifty people round a banana tree which grew at the back of one of the huts, and with much shouting they pointed out the snake to us. It was coiled in and out of a very large bunch of bananas at the top of the tree, and it surveyed us with a glittering eye. John asked me if it was poisonous, and I replied that, so far as I could see, it was a tree viper of sorts, and probably quite poisonous enough to make things interesting should it bite anyone. John retreated as far as the crowds would let him, and asked how I proposed to capture it. As far as I could see the best way was to cut down the bunch of bananas with the snake inside, and so we carefully ringed the area in which the fruit would fall, with the smallest mesh net we possessed, and I stationed John on the outside of this, armed with a stick to repel the snake should it try to get away. Then I borrowed a machete off a bystander, and asked the crowd if the owner of the tree would mind my cutting down the unripe fruit. Several voices assured me that he would not mind at all, and it was only later, when the real owner turned up, that I found out he objected very strongly and to the tune of several shillings. However, I approached the tree swinging my machete in a professional manner. The crowd had now increased considerably, and we were surrounded by a solid wedge of humanity all anxious to watch the white man's snake-catching methods. When I discovered that I could not reach the bananas to cut the stem, they were all greatly amused.

"I shall have to cut the whole tree down," I said to John.

"All right," he replied, "only wish we could get rid of this crowd. If the damn thing makes a run for it someone will get bitten."

"Don't worry," I said soothingly, "if it does make a run for it they'll get out of the way quickly enough."

I started to hack at the trunk of the tree. Now, the stem of a banana tree is deceptive: it looks quite solid, but in reality it is soft and fibrous and juicy, and very easily cut. This I did not know, so it was with considerable surprise that I felt the blade of the machete go right through the trunk at my second swipe, and the whole tree crashed earthwards. That it should fall exactly where John was standing was pure bad luck. With an agility of which I would not have thought him capable, he leapt to one side, and the tree missed him. The bunch of bananas was broken off by the fall and rolled and bounced its way across the ground to his feet, and the snake fell from it, wiggling angrily. The crowd, as I had predicted, faded away, and John was left facing the angry snake with nothing between them but a length of flimsy net.

Apparently I had misjudged the size of the snake, for he proceeded to wiggle through the net with the greatest of ease, and then, before John could do anything to prevent it, it slithered between his legs and off into the undergrowth. It was useless to search for him in that thick mass of bushes, so I started to disentangle the net from the wreck of the banana tree. John watched me malevolently.

"I have decided", he said at last, "that I am not cut out for this snake-charming stuff. In future you can catch all snakes yourself."

"But they seem to like you," I pointed out, "you fascinate them. Now, if we could only hang some nets round your legs, all the snakes rushing to get close to you would become entangled. You ought to be flattered, it's not everyone that has this magnetic attraction for reptiles."

"Thank you," said John witheringly, "your suggestion about the nets, though I've no doubt it's very sound, would, I feel, hamper my movements somewhat; I am quite happy exercising a fascination over birds, without enlarging my repertoire to include reptiles." Then he stalked up the hill and left me to interview the owner of the banana tree who had just arrived.

The last affair came three days later. A voluble hunter arrived carrying a small basket in which nestled a fat and beautiful Gaboon Viper. The skin of these plump, squat-looking snakes is covered with the most intricate and colourful pattern, and having purchased it, I carried it in for John to admire. The reptile had recently shed his skin, so the colours glowed with life, a lovely patchwork of pink, red, fawn, silver, and chocolate. John admired it, but implored me to keep it safely locked up.

"It's deadly, isn't it, old boy?" he asked.

"Yes, very deadly."

"Well, for goodness' sake keep it in its cage ... remember the water-snakes. We don't want a repetition of that."

"Don't worry, I'm having a special cage built for it."

So the special cage was built, and the sluggish and deadly viper placed reverently inside. All would have been well if it had not been for the thunderstorm. This broke with unusual force just as I was having my bath and, remembering that the reptile cages were piled out in the open, I yelled to the animal staff to bring them in. If the cages got damp the wood warped and it is surprising how small a crack a snake can squeeze through if it wants to. The cages were rushed inside and piled up near the monkeys. This proved my undoing.

John was seated near the table, in his pyjamas: he was busy cutting down some old fruit tins to make into water

Gaboon Viper

pots for the birds, and he was absorbed in his work. I was just putting the finishing touches to my toilet when I saw something move in the shadows beneath his chair. Putting on my dressing-gown I went closer to see what it was. There on the floor, about six inches away from John's inadequately slippered feet, lay the Gaboon Viper. I had always believed, judging by what I had read and was told, that at moments like this one should speak quietly to the victim, thus avoiding panic and sudden movement. So, clearing my throat, I spoke calmly and gently:

"Keep quite still, old boy, the Gaboon Viper is under your chair."

On looking back I feel that I should have left out any reference to the snake in my request. As it was my remark had an extraordinary and arresting effect on my companion. He left the chair with a speed and suddenness that was startling, and suggestive of the better examples of levitation. The tin can, the hammer, and the tin cutters, went flying in various parts of the hut, and the supper table was all but overturned. The Gaboon Viper, startled by all this activity, shot out from under the chair and wiggled determinedly towards the back of the monkey cages. I headed him off, and after a few tense minutes got him entangled in the folds of a butterfly-net, then I carried him and dumped him in his cage. I saw then the reason for his escape: the reptiles had been stacked too close to the monkeys, and a female Drill had amused herself by putting her paws through the bars and undoing all the cages she could reach. The first one, as always happens, belonged to the Gaboon Viper. John said little, but it was terse and to the point. I agreed with him wholeheartedly for, should the snake have bitten him he would not have survived: there was no snake-bite serum in the Cameroons, to the best of my knowledge, and the nearest doctor was twenty-five miles away, and we had no transport.

"Why don't you go away again?" asked John plaintively. "It's at least three weeks since you came back from Eshobi, high time you plunged back into the impenetrable bush in search of more beef."

"Well," I said thoughtfully, "I had thought of going off again, if you don't mind holding the fort."

"Where were you thinking of going?"

"N'da Ali," I replied.

"Good Lord, that's an idea. You might even get killed on one of those cliffs with a bit of luck," said John cheerfully.

N'da Ali was the largest mountain in the vicinity. It crouched at our backs, glowering over the landscape, the village, and our little hill. From almost every vantage point you were aware of the mountains' mist-entangled, cloud-veiled shape brooding over everything, its heights guarded by sheer cliffs of gnarled granite so steep that no plant

life could get a foothold. Every day I had looked longingly at the summit, and every day I had watched N'da Ali
in her many moods. In the early morning she was a great
mist-whitened monster; at noon she was all green and golden
glitter of forest, her cliffs flushing pink in the sun; at night
she was purple and shapeless, fading to black as the sun sank.
Sometimes she would go into hiding, drawing the white
clouds around herself and brooding in their depths for two
or three days at a time. Every day I gazed at those great
cliffs that guarded the way to the thick forest on her ridged
back, and each day I grew more determined that I would
go up there and see what she had to offer me. Since John
seemed so anxious to get rid of me I lost little time in making
enquiries. I found out that N'da Ali really belonged to the
people of a neighbouring village called Fineschang, and
naturally the mountain had a *ju-ju* on it. No self-respecting
mountain like N'da Ali would be without its *ju-ju*. Further
investigation disclosed the fact that, while the people of
Fineschang were allowed, by the terms of the *ju-ju* (if I may
put it like that), to hunt and fish on the lower slopes of the
mountain, only one man was allowed access to the summit.
It transpired that there was only one way up to the summit
anyhow, and this particular man was the only one who knew
it. So I sent him a message saying I would be pleased if he
would take me up N'da Ali for the day to look out for a suitable camp site. Then when this had been arranged, if he
would accompany my troupe of hunters, bird-trappers, and
hangers on to the top and superintend the whole affair.
While I waited with ill-concealed impatience for his reply, I
gazed all the more longingly at the slopes of the mountain.

John's bird collection was now of impressive dimensions,
and was more than a full-time job. Apart from the preparations of food (hard-boiled eggs, chopping up cooked meat,
soaking dried fruit, and so on), he would move from cage to
cage with a tin full of grasshoppers or wasp grubs and a pair
of tweezers, and solemnly feed each bird individually. In
this way he was sure that every specimen was feeding properly, and was getting the required amount of live food to keep

it healthy. His patience and painstaking methods were a joy to watch, and under his care the birds prospered and sang happily in their wooden cages. His chief source of annoyance were the maimed and dying birds that were brought in to him. He would come to me holding in his hands a colourful and lovely bird, and show it to me. "Look at this, old boy," he would say angrily, "a beautiful thing, and absolutely useless just because these blasted people can't take care in handling them. It's quite useless, got a broken wing. Really, it's enough to make you weep." He would go off and the following conversation would take place with the hunter.

"This bird no good," John would say, "it get wound. It go die."

"No, sah," the hunter would reply, "he no get wound, sah."

"It's got a broken wing, you hold it too tight," John would say.

"No, sah, he no fit die, sah. Na good bird, sah."

"What can you do with these fools?" John would say, turning to me, "they always assure me the thing won't die, even if it's got every bone in its body broken."

"I know, they try their best to persuade you."

"But it's so annoying. I would have given him five bob for this if it had been in good condition. But even if you explain that they don't seem to see it. They're hopeless."

One day a hunter turned up carrying a Crested Guineafowl, a bird as large as a chicken, with a blue-grey plumage covered with white spots, and its head adorned with a crest of curly black feathers. It seemed to be in very bad condition, and after examining it, John agreed that it was not long for this world.

"I no buy him. He go die," said John.

The hunter appeared cut to the quick at this disparaging remark.

"No, sah," he gasped, "he no go die. Na strong bird dis. I go show Masa," and he placed the bird on the floor. Just as he was protesting for the second time that it would not die, the Guinea-fowl rolled over, gave a couple of kicks and expired. It was a very crestfallen hunter who went off down the hill with our laughter following him, and shouted jeers from the animal staff.

Shortly before this John had been brought another of these guinea-fowl, together with the clutch of eight eggs she had been sitting on when she was captured. After some trouble we found a broody hen in the village, and purchased it. She sat well on the Guinea-fowl's eggs and in due course

Sclater's Crested Guinea-fowl

hatched them all out. The young were delightful, if drab, little things, and scuttled around the pen in which their foster-mother was confined as ordinary chicks will. Unfortunately their hen mother was a great, muscular, heavy-footed bird, and was constantly treading on her offspring. She was very proud of them, but would walk over them with complete unconcern, and a bland expression on her face. In desperation John tried to get another foster parent, built on less generous lines, with more grace of movement, but all in vain.

153

The great, clumsy hen slowly but surely trod on all the delicate little Guinea-fowl, and killed the lot. Later, John was brought another clutch of eggs, and even found a more sylph-like hen to sit on them, but they must have been in the hunter's hands for some time, or else he had handled them roughly and damaged them, for they never hatched. John was depressed by this bad luck for, although he had six female Guinea-fowl, he wanted to get at least one male so that he could take a breeding stock back to England, and there, under ideal conditions in aviaries with slim and delicate bantams or silkys to hatch and rear, the birds could be bred.

There was one dreadful period when an epidemic of mycosis ran like fire through his bird cages, killing some of his most choice specimens. This disease is a deadly thing, a peculiar fungus-like growth which develops in the bird's lungs, spreads with incredible speed through other organs, and kills the bird rapidly. There is apparently no sign of this complaint until the later stages, when you will see the bird breathing heavily, as though it had a cold. But by this time it is too late to do anything effective. When this horrible disease took a hold on the bird collection, John fought it in every possible way, but still the losses increased. He was losing specimens which had taken months to obtain, and could not be replaced. He told me that there was only one thing which could possibly have any effect on the disease, and that was potassium iodide. Where we were to obtain this commodity in the middle of the Cameroon forest was the question. Now, there was a small hospital at Mamfe, and hither I went in search of the required drug, but discovered that they had none. That seemed to be that, and my hopes of John saving his collection dwindled to nothing. I happened to be buying some things in the United Africa Company's store when I came across a row of dusty bottles piled in a dark corner of the shop. On examining them I discovered, with astonishment and incredulity, that they were a dozen good bottles with potassium iodide written on the label. I went in search of the manager.

"Those bottles down in the store, are they really potassium iodide?" I asked of him eagerly.

"Yes, blasted stuff. They sent it up from Calabar on the last canoe. I can't think what for, because I can't sell the stuff," he replied.

"Well, you've just sold the lot," I said jubilantly.

"What in the name of Heaven do you want with a dozen bottles?" asked the manager, considerably astonished.

I explained at great length.

"But are you sure you want the whole dozen? It's an awful lot of potassium iodide, you know."

"If something isn't done we shan't have any birds left," I said, "and I'm not going to take too little and then find, when I come back for more, that you've sold out, or something. No, I'll take the whole lot. How much are they?"

The manager named a price that I would have thought expensive for an iron lung, but I had to have those bottles. Carefully they were packed in the lorry, and I drove back to John in high spirits.

"I've got you some potassium iodide, old boy," I said on arrival, "so now there is no excuse for killing your specimens off."

"Oh, good work," said John, and then he gaped at the box I presented to him, "is that *all* potassium iodide?"

"Yes, I thought I might as well get a supply in. I wasn't sure how much you would need. Is it enough?"

"Enough?" said John faintly. "There is enough of the stuff here to last fifty collectors approximately two hundred years."

And so it proved. For months afterwards our baggage was full of bottles of potassium iodide. We couldn't get rid of the stuff. It hung about and seized every opportunity of upsetting itself on our clean shirts, or cunningly mixing itself with the bicarbonate of soda. But it checked the mycosis, and that was the main thing.

By this time I had almost forgotten about the hunter I had sent the message to about N'da Ali, and I was quite surprised when a messenger appeared one morning from Fineschang. The hunter, I learned, would be very pleased to lead me on a day reconnaissance of the mountain, at any time that would suit me. I decided on a day and sent a message back to say that I would be at Fineschang on that morning. I also sent a packet of cigarettes and a bottle of beer, in case the *ju-ju* should think that I had overlooked it.

"Ah!" said John, when he heard the news, "so you are going on Thursday. Do you think you are going to be able to get up to the top and back in one day?"

We both looked at the almost sheer cliffs of N'da Ali gleaming pinkly in the evening sun.

"I think so," I replied, "at any rate, I'm going to have a damn good try.

CHAPTER NINE

Arctocebus Ahoy!

The day appointed for my mountaineering arrived and dawned bright and clear. N'da Ali was invisible behind a wall of mist; everywhere the forest smoked and steamed, and small hills would appear suddenly out of the mist, like misshapen ships in a fog. What could be seen of the forest was gleaming golden-green in the pale morning sunlight.

I had gaily agreed to be at Fineschang at eleven o'clock. It had not occurred to me until the night before that I had no means of getting to my destination except by walking, and as Fineschang was ten miles away along a hot and dusty road, this idea was uninteresting. Frantic last-minute conferences with the staff had disclosed the fact that a district messenger was staying in the village, and he had with him a shiny new bicycle. The messenger was most helpful, and agreed to lend me his machine; so in the morning sun the great, heavy bicycle was solemnly wheeled up to our hut, and I prepared to depart. I had decided to take Daniel with me, as he was the smallest and lightest of the animal staff, and so could be accommodated on the crossbar. Apart from this passenger I had a large bag of collecting gear, and another one full of sandwiches and beer to sustain me on the journey. As I was tying these on the bicycle John appeared on the scene.

"Why are you taking all that beer?" he inquired.

"Well, to begin with, it's going to be thirsty work shin-

157

ning up that mountain, and apart from that I've found that beer has a very soothing effect on *ju-jus* and their owners."

Daniel approached and eyed me nervously. It was obvious that he had very little faith in my cycling abilities.

"Where I go sit, sah?" he asked.

"Here on the crossbar," I said.

I leant forward and hauled him up. He clutched wildly at the handlebars and twisted them round, and we fell to the ground in a tangled heap, amid the clanking of beer bottles.

"This does not look to me like the start of a scientific expedition," said John gravely, "it looks more like an elopement."

I righted the machine and hauled Daniel aboard, this time without mishap. We wobbled off down the path.

"Bye bye, old boy," called John earnestly.

"'Bye . . ." I yelled, steering cautiously round the pot-holes.

"See you to-night," called John, with complete lack of conviction.

We sped down the hill and shot out on to the high road like a drunken snipe. Here I found the going easier, but my chief difficulty was to get Daniel to loosen his vice-like grip on the handlebars so that I could steer with greater accuracy. Cycling along a Cameroon road is an unforgettable experience: the rich, silky red dust spreads upwards in great clouds enveloping you and your machine; pot-holes of great depth and jagged edges loom suddenly under your front wheel, making you swerve wildly back and forth across the road; every hundred yards or so you come suddenly upon an area which has been liberally sprinkled with rocks of various sizes, and riding across these you feel that a fractured pelvis is the least you can hope to sustain. Every half-mile you crossed a bridge: these consisted of two thick beams laid from bank to bank, with planks laid crossways or, in some cases, lengthways. It was one of the latter type I was silly enough to try and ride over quite early in the trip. My front tyre slid delightedly into the groove between the two planks and stuck there and Daniel, the beer, and I, fell to the ground. By now the sun had come out from the mist and the heat on the open road was terrific. By the time we had reached the half-way mark I was pouring with sweat, and my mouth and eyes were clogged with dust. We swept down a hill, and at the bottom was the inevitable bridge, spanning a wide, shallow stream, with snow-white sandbanks and tall trees grouped round it casting deep shadows. I weakened.

"We go stop here small time, Daniel," I said hoarsely, "sometime there go be beef for this small water."

I knew perfectly well that there would be no beef of importance in such a place, but I wanted to soak in the clear glinting waters and get some of the dust off my body. We left the cycle in the ditch and made our way down the slope to the water, where we stripped and plunged in, and watched the red dust washed from our bodies like swirls of blood in the clear waters. Half an hour later we were still sitting in the shallows, relaxed and cool with the waters playing over us, when I suddenly saw a strange thing, which immediately roused me out of my trance. A long brown ribbon of water weed which was attached to the rock near me, detached itself suddenly and swam away. I gazed after it in astonishment, then floundered to my feet with a cry and started in pursuit. The weed swam quickly upstream and went to earth under a small boulder. With Daniel's aid I shifted the stone and we captured this piece of aquatic flora. Cupped in my hands I held the most extraordinary fish. It was long, narrow, thin, and brown, exactly like a long ribbon of weed. Its face was pulled out into a little snout, and its eyes were round and staring, but they seemed to have more intelligence in them than any ordinary fish's. I recognized it because I had spent many happy hours hunting its relatives in the weed beds in the southern Mediterranean. It was a Pipe-fish. I was astonished, for I had not expected to find a freshwater pipe fish pretending to be a bit of water weed in an African river. I fashioned a small pool for it and placed it inside. It at once fastened itself to a small rock and turned into a bit of weed, curving and shimmering with the current. I pondered over it unhappily: I longed to know what its habits were, where it laid its eggs and hatched its young, and a hundred other things about it, but I realized mournfully, and not for the first time, that when you are collecting for a living you cannot spend your time unravelling the life history of an obscure fish. Reluctantly, annoyed at the harshness of life, I released the Pipe-fish and watched it swim off into deep water. But the capture of the fish had roused me out of my dream-like trance.

We left the river and returned to the road, and remounted the bicycle which, by now, I was beginning to dislike intensely. I pounded miserably onwards, feeling the dust settling once more on my body and clothes.

Half an hour later we were free-wheeling down a long gentle incline, when I saw a figure in the distance marching towards us. As we drew closer I saw that the man was carrying a small basket fashioned out of green palm leaves, a sure sign that he was bringing an animal to sell.

"Dat man get beef, Daniel?" I asked, putting on the brakes.

"I tink so, sah."

The man came padding along the dusty road, and as he drew closer he doffed his cap and grinned, and I recognized him as an Eshobi hunter.

"Welcome," I called. "You done come?"

"Morning, sah!" he answered, holding out his green basket. "I done bring beef for Masa."

"Well, I hope it's good beef," I said, as I took it, "or else you've walked a long way for nothing."

Daniel and the hunter shook hands and chattered away in Banyangi while I undid the mouth of the basket and peered inside.

I don't know what I expected to see: a Pouched rat, or possibly a squirrel, certainly nothing very unusual. But there, blinking up at me out of great golden eyes from the bottom of the basket, was an Angwantibo!

There are certain exquisite moments in life which should be enjoyed to the full, for, unfortunately, they are rare. I certainly made the most of this one, for both Daniel and the hunter thought I had gone mad. I executed a war dance in the middle of the road, I whooped so loudly in my excitement that I sent all the hornbills for miles around honking into the forest. I slapped the hunter on the back, I slapped Daniel on the back, and I would, if I could have managed it, have slapped myself on the back. After all those months of searching and failure I held a real live Angwantibo in my hands, and delight at the thought went to my head like wine.

Angwantibo

"Which day you done catch this beef?" I asked, as soon as my excitement had died down somewhat.

"Yesterday, sah, for night-time."

That meant that the precious creature had been without food and water for twenty-four hours. It was imperative that I got it back to Bakebe immediately and gave it something to eat and drink.

"Daniel, I go ride quickly-quickly to Bakebe to give dis

beef some chop. You go follow with dis hunter-man, you hear?"

"Yes, sah."

I loaded him down with the collecting gear and the beer, and then I hung the basket containing the Angwantibo round my neck and set off along the road to Bakebe. I sped along like a swallow, taking dust, pot-holes, and bridges in my stride and not even noticing them. My one desire was to get the priceless little beast now hanging round my neck into a decent cage, with an adequate supply of fruit and milk. Bakebe was reached at last, and, leaving the cycle in the village, I panted up the hill towards our hut. Half-way up a dreadful thought occurred to me: maybe my identification had been too rapid, maybe it wasn't an Angwantibo after all, but merely a young Potto, and an animal very similar in appearance. With a sinking heart I opened the basket and peered at the animal again. Quickly I checked identification of various parts of its furry anatomy: shape and number of fingers on its hands, size of ears, lack of tail. No, it really was an Angwantibo. Heaving a sigh of relief I continued on my way.

As I came within sight of the hut I could see John moving along the row of cages, feeding his birds; bursting with pride and excitement I bellowed out the good news to him, waving my hat furiously and breaking into a run:

"John, I've got one . . . an Angwantibo . . . alive and kicking. . . . An ANGWANTIBO, d'you hear?"

At this all the staff, both animal and household, dashed out to meet me and see this beef that I had talked about incessantly for so long, and for which I had offered such a fantastic price. They all grinned and jabbered at my obvious delight and excitement. John, on the other hand, displayed complete lack of interest in the earth-shaking event; he merely glanced over his shoulder and said, "Good show, old boy," and continued to feed his birds. I could have quite cheerfully kicked him had not my pleasure been so great.

No other animal's arrival had created half the upheaval that the Angwantibo's did: a family of Pouched rats that were sleeping peacefully in their cage were routed out unceremoniously, and the cage was swept and cleaned as a temporary abode for the creature. The carpenter was given a big box and told to produce, in record time, the biggest and best cage he could construct, or else suffer a dreadful fate. Various members of the staff were sent scurrying in all directions to procure eggs, pawpaw, banana, and dead birds. At last, when the cage had been furnished with a nice set of branches, and there were plates of food and drink on the clean sawdust floor, the great moment came. With a thick crowd around me, hardly daring to breathe in case they disturbed this valuable animal and thus earned my wrath, I carefully tipped the Angwantibo out of the basket and into his temporary home. He stood on the floor for a moment, looking about him; then he walked over to one of the plates, seized a bit of banana in his mouth, and then climbed swiftly up into the branches, and crouching there commenced to eat the fruit greedily. This was a very pleasant surprise; after my experiences with other nervous creatures I had not expected him to eat at once. As I watched him sitting in the branch mumbling his banana I felt quite unreasonably proud, as though I had captured him myself.

"John," I called in a hoarse whisper, "come and see him."

"Oh, he's quite a pretty little animal," he said.

This was the highest praise you could get out of John for anything without feathers. And indeed, he was a pretty little animal. He looked not unlike a teddy-bear, with his thick golden-brown fur, his curved back, and golden eyes. He was about the size of a four-week-old kitten, and though his body was fat and furry enough, his legs, in proportion, seemed long and slender. His hands and feet were extraordinarily like a human's, except that on his hands the first and second fingers had been reduced to mere stumps. This, of course, gave him a much greater grasping power, for without the first two fingers in the way he could get his little hands round quite a thick branch, and once having got a grip he would cling on as though glued.

After I had stood in silent and awed contemplation of the

beast for half an hour, during which time he ate one and a half bananas, he scrambled on to a suitably sloping branch, grasped it firmly with hands and feet, tucked his head between his front legs, his forehead resting on the wood, and went to sleep. Reverently I covered the cage with a cloth so that the sunlight should not disturb him, and tip-toed away.

Every half-hour or so I would creep back to the cage and peep at him to make sure that he had not dropped down dead or been spirited away by some powerful *ju-ju*, and for the first two days I would leap out of bed in the morning and rush to his cage, even before imbibing my morning cup of tea, a most unheard of event. John also became infected with my nervousness, and would peer out from under his mos- quito-net like a woodpecker from its hole and watch me anxiously as I removed the sacking from the cage front and looked inside.

"Is it all right?" he would inquire. "Has it eaten?"

"Yes, half a banana and the whole of that dead bird."

Now, there were several reasons for the fuss that was made over the Angwantibo, or, to give it its correct title, *Arctocebus calabarensis*. The first was that the animal is ex- tremely rare, being found only in the forests of the British and French Cameroons, and even here they do not seem common. The second reason was that they had long been wanted by the London Zoo, and they had asked us specially to try and obtain them a specimen.

Though the Angwantibo had been known to science since 1859, the British Museum have still only some dozen speci- mens of it, and all naturalists who have searched for the ani- mal in its native haunts agree that it is extremely rare and hard to find. The Angwantibo is a lemuroid, a group of ani- mals closely related to the monkeys. Only once before had this little creature been kept alive in captivity and studied, but this was the first time that anyone had tried to bring one back alive to England. If we were successful it meant that for the first time zoologists and anatomists would be able to ob- serve the habits and movement of a live Angwantibo. So, naturally, we weren't taking any chances with losing the one we had, for we thought it might well be the only one we should get.

I will give this little fellow his due and state that he was no trouble at all. At once he showed a preference for bananas and the plump breast of a dead bird. This he would wash down with a drink of milk. Then he would have a light snack of half a dozen grasshoppers just before we went to bed. All day he would sleep, clinging tightly to the branch, his head buried between his front legs. In the evening, just before sunset, he would wake up, give himself a rapid grooming, yawn once or twice, showing his bright pink tongue, and then he would start on his stroll about the cage to work up an appetite. He would climb down one side of the cage, walk across the floor to the other side, hoist himself into the branches, scramble along them until he was back where he started, and then repeat the whole performance over again. This little circular tour he would continue for about an hour, until it was time to feed. As soon as his plate was put in he would start to eat, showing no sign of fear at all. Sometimes he would come down and stand on the floor, his head hanging low and his back humped up, looking more like a miniature bear than ever. Occasionally, if his plate was placed directly under a convenient branch, he would hang down by his feet, and grab the pieces of banana with his pink hands and stuff them into his mouth, smacking his lips and licking the juice from his nose. During all the time that I had him I never heard him make any noise except a cat-like growl and a faint hissing when I tried to handle him. To get him off a branch required considerable effort, for with his queer misshapen hands and feet he would grip the branch with incredible strength. To get him off you were forced to grab him round the chest and pull, and he would counter this by ducking his head between his front legs and biting you in the thumb with his needle-sharp teeth.

After a week, when I was sure that Arcto, as we called him, had thoroughly settled down, I again attempted my reconnaisance of N'da Ali. Once again Daniel and I rode through the dust and pot-holes, but this time we were not turned back, and we arrived hot and dishevelled at Fine-schang round about eleven one morning. I found the hunter awaiting me, and a more surly, objectionable character I have never met. Apart from his face, which left much to be desired, his feet were swollen to twice normal size with elephantiasis, and he had those peculiar patches all over his legs which you sometimes see among the natives: areas like large birth-marks which are devoid of the natural brown pigment, and are a horrible pale pink, with the surface of the skin shiny like patent leather. We started without delay, leaving Daniel in the village, for I thought that such a climb would be too much for one so young and of such frail physique. It wasn't until we were half-way up that I discovered my own physical condition left much to be desired.

The hunter walked up the slope of the mountain, which appeared to be a gradient of two in one, at a tremendous speed, and I scrambled behind with the sweat pouring down my face, doing my best to uphold the White Man's prestige. Only once did the hunter check his speed, and that was at one point where a green mamba, probably the fastest and most deadly of West African snakes, whisked across our path like a streak of green lightning. It appeared round the trunk of one tree, wiggled across the path some three feet in front of the hunter's misshapen feet, and disappeared among the bushes; the hunter stopped dead and went a pale cheese colour. He gazed ferociously in the direction the reptile had taken, and then turned to me:

"Ugh!" he said vehemently and comprehensively. It was the only remark he had made since we started, so I felt I ought to be sociable.

"Ugh!" I agreed.

We continued upwards in silence.

When we had reached the half-way mark the hunter led me to a large shallow pool at the base of the waterfall, and here he removed his sarong and proceeded to bathe. I did likewise, choosing a position upstream from him as I had no particular desire to catch any of the great variety of diseases he was suffering from. When he had washed he drank vigorously, belching in between gulps . . . a remarkable and sustained performance. I squatted on a rock to open a bottle of beer; it was then that I discovered the opener had been left behind. Offering a brief prayer for the soul of the person who had packed the bag, I broke the neck off the bottle and drank gratefully, hoping that there was not too much glass inside. The hunter had now disappeared behind some rock, with becoming modesty, and was performing what appeared to be, to judge from the noise he was making, his annual catharsis. Not wishing to intrude on so private and, it seemed, so painful a matter, I amused myself by wandering among the rocks at the base of the falls, in search of frogs.

Eventually my guide reappeared and we went on our way. After a time I walked in a sort of trance, the sweat running down into my eyes unheeded. That part of the trip seems to be a complete blank. I came to as we burst out of the forest into a tiny grass field, bleached white by the sun, and a troupe of Mona Guenons rushed from the grass and leapt into the trees with a crashing of leaves. We could hear them crashing off, shouting "oink . . . oink . . . ," to each other, as Monas do. The hunter led me to the edge of the grass field where there was an enormous rock, as big as a house, perched on the edge of the cliff we had just climbed. Scrambling to the top of this a wonderful sight met my eyes.

In every direction stretched the forest below us, miles and miles of undulating country, here and there rising into a curious shaped hill, all of it covered with a thick pelt of trees in every shade and combination of greens. Far away below us, like a faint chalk stripe among the trees lay the road, and following it along with my eyes I could see Bakebe, and perched on the hill above, the big hut that housed our collection. In front of us the forest rolled away to the French border and beyond, and to our right, seen dimly shimmering in the heat haze, more like a faint fingerprint on the blue sky, I could see Mount Cameroon, nearly eighty miles away. It was a breath-taking and beautiful sight, and for the first time I fully realized the vastness of the incredible forest. From the plain below where we sat the forest stretched, almost unbroken, right across Africa, until it merged into the savannah land of the east: Kenya, Tanganyika, and Rhodesia. It was an astonishing thought. I sat there smoking a much needed cigarette, and wondering how many beef there were to a square mile, but after a few minutes of intense mental arithmetic I began to feel dizzy at the thought of such numbers and I gave it up.

The hunter lay on the rock and went to sleep. I sat there and examined a vast area of forest with the aid of my field-glasses, and I found it a fascinating occupation. I followed the flight of the hornbills across the tops of the trees which, from this distance, resembled the head of a cauliflower: I watched a troupe of monkeys, only visible by the movement of the leaves as they jumped from tree to tree.

Along the road a speck that looked like an exotic red beetle became the Mamfe to Kumba lorry, apparently creeping along the road and dragging a plume of dust behind it. I followed it along for quite some time and then switched to something else, which was a pity, as half a mile further on the lorry went through a bridge and dropped twenty feet into the river below, a thing I did not learn about until I returned home and found that John had spent the afternoon administering first aid to the wounded passengers.

As the hunter was slumbering peacefully I at last climbed down from the rock and explored the grass field. On the opposite side, some twenty feet into the trees, I came upon a glade between the great tree trunks, and here a tiny stream meandered its way through moss-covered boulders. This, I decided, was the very place for a camp. When I had examined the ground, peered under a few boulders, and generally investigated the position, I walked on through the forest, and presently came to another grass field, much larger than the first. So apparently the camp site I had chosen was in a tongue of forest, bordered on two sides by grass. This struck me as admirable, for I felt that these grass fields might well yield some good specimens.

Returning, I found the hunter awake, and I suggested that we should now return as I had seen all I wanted to see, and it was getting late. He led the way without a word; he was by far the most silent inhabitant of the Cameroons I had come across. The way down was much easier, and so we made better time. As we reached the last slope of the mountain a sudden wind sprang up, bringing with it a sharp shower of rain. Leaves and small branches were ripped from the trees and fell all about us, and somewhere in the forest we heard a splintering crash that denoted the fall of quite a large branch or tree, bent beyond endurance by this sudden fierce wind.

We arrived at Fineschang wet through, and I took shelter in the hunter's evil-smelling abode, where presently Daniel joined me. After we had smoked for a while the hunter showed no signs of broaching the subject, so I asked him when he would lead my party up the mountain and pitch the camp, and how much he would want for the job.

"Masa go pay me twenty pounds for do dis ting," he stated calmly.

I was so surprised I laughed, which seemed to annoy him, for he went into a long tirade about the *ju-ju* that lived on the mountain over which he was the only man to have any control, and what a dangerous business it was placating a *ju-ju*, and so on. Then he really nettled me by stating that I could not go up the mountain without him, so I would have to accept his price. It had stopped raining, so I rose to my feet and glared at him.

"Listen, my friend, if you go take me for dis place I go pay you two shillings a day, and I go dash you when I come back if I catch good beef up dere. If you no agree, I go for dis place myself. I go get other hunter man who go help me, you hear? If you agree, tell me."

The hunter looked at me scornfully and said something derogatory in his own language, to which Daniel replied heatedly.

"Does he agree, Daniel?"

"No, sah, he no agree."

"Come, then, we go leave dis stupid man," I said. I laid three shillings on the step of his house and strode out of the village wrathfully, mounted the bicycle with all the dignity I could muster, and rode away.

CHAPTER TEN

N'da Ali

We started for N'da Ali at some hideous grey hour in the morning, and by the time the sun had broken through the mists we had reached the lower slopes of the mountain. It was a hard climb from then on, and the carriers moaned and whistled and gasped as they crawled their way upwards, hoisting themselves and their loads from rock to rock, and edging their way over and around the great curled tree roots. It was in this type of country more than in any other that I felt a great respect and sympathy for my carriers. Here was I, unencumbered except for field-glasses and a shotgun, gasping for breath and feeling my heart pounding as though it would burst, having to sit down every half-mile or so for a rest. Yet the line of carriers crawled steadily upwards with their great loads balanced on their woolly heads, their faces gleaming with sweat, and their neck muscles standing out with the effort of supporting and balancing the boxes and bales. The Tailor and I moved ahead and above them, picking out the easiest path for them to travel, and the Tailor marking it with quick cuts of his machete into the green bark of the saplings. When we came to a place where the rocks were dangerous, or a huge tree lay across our path in a shroud of lianas, the Tailor and I would pause and wait for the carriers to catch up so that we could help them over the obstacle. As each carrier passed I would exchange a remark in pidgin with him, much to the amusement of the others.

"Iseeya, bo."

"Tank you, Masa. . . ."

"You get power too much, my friend."

"Na true, sah."

"Walka strong, bo."

"I go try, Masa."

And so on as each grinning, sweating man negotiated the difficult area. On reaching the other side in safety each man would whistle sharply through his teeth, a great exhalation of breath that echoed briefly through the trees.

After an hour's steady climbing I judged that we were about half-way to our objective, the place I had chosen for the camp site, and so I called a halt on a comparatively flat area of land. The carriers put down their loads with grunts of relief and squatted round on their haunches breathing deeply, while the Tailor distributed the cigarettes I had brought for them. Half an hour later the men rewound the little mats of leaf or cloth which they place on their heads, the loads were hoisted up again, and we set off on the last lap of the journey.

We had started up the lower slope of N'da Ali at seven-thirty, and by eleven we had reached the flat area of forest that represented the great "step" that ran along one side of the mountain. It was not long before we passed through a small grass field, and on the other side we entered a thin woodland bordering on a small stream. Here the loads were put down and great activity took place: the tent was erected, a kitchen was made out of saplings and grass, and the carriers built themselves tiny, goblin-like houses among the tall buttress roots of a huge tree nearby. When some sort of order had been established the Tailor, myself, and the youth who was to act as bird trapper, went into the neighbouring forest and picked out and marked some thirty spots that seemed likely places for setting traps. Then the youth was sent off to cut himself the twigs and branches for trap building. Having got this under control I wandered off by myself, following the course of a tiny stream that glinted and purred its way through the mossy boulders twenty feet from my tent, in the hopes of finding a place deep enough to bathe in. Soon I found the stream entered a thick tangle of low undergrowth, and here it flowed over a great sheet of rock, which it had hollowed out into a series of pools. The largest of these was some fifteen feet long, and about two feet deep: it was lined with a bed of white sand and a scattering of small smooth yellow pebbles. As a natural bathtub it left nothing to be desired, and I stripped and stepped gratefully into the water. The shock I received was considerable, for the streams in the lowlands, though cold, were not unpleasant. But this stream was pure snow-broth that numbed sensation and

Serval

made the extremities of your body ache. I splashed half-heartedly for a few minutes and then climbed out with my teeth chattering, and gathering up my shoes and clothes I made my way through the undergrowth into the grass field. After assuring myself that there was nothing more dangerous than a few locusts about, I stretched myself in the sun to dry.

I dozed for a time, and presently I sat up and looked about me: not thirty feet away from me, among the golden tufts of grass, stood a handsome spotted cat gazing at me with an expression of meditative appraisal. For one frightful moment

I thought it was a leopard, but a longer look and I recognized it as a Serval, an animal much smaller, and with a brownish coat covered with small round spots. My chief feeling was one of surprise, for every hunter, black or white, and nearly every book that has been written about the forest assures one that if you catch a glimpse of a great cat once in fifty years you are doing fine. So I was filled with a mixture of apprehension and pleasure on finding the Serval there when I awoke.

It stood quite still, regarding me thoughtfully, and the tip of its tail moved very gently among the grass stalks. I had seen domestic cats looking like this at sparrows, twitching their tails, and I did not feel very happy about it. Also, I was stark naked, and I have found that in moments of crisis to have no clothes on gives one a terribly unprotected feeling. I glared at the Serval, wishing that I had my shorts on and that I could think of some way of capturing it without the risk of being disembowelled. The Serval blinked its eyes and looked as though it was considering lying down in the warm grass and joining me in a nap. Just at that moment an uproar broke out from the direction of the camp, and the cat, after glancing hurriedly over its shoulder in the direction of the noise, disappeared into the undergrowth with a swift smooth rush. I struggled hastily into my shorts and shoes, and although I was not long in reaching the spot where the cat had entered the bushes, I could see no sign of it. In the warm, still air there hung a strong, pungent odour, and in the patch of soft earth was one paw mark. Cursing myself, the carriers, and the Serval with equal vehemence, I made my way back to camp, and here I found out the reason for the noise that had startled the cat. One side of the kitchen had collapsed, and everyone was standing around arguing and shouting, while the cook, his hair full of grass, was dancing with rage. I took the Tailor aside, out of earshot of the more timid members of my retinue, and told him what I had just seen.

"It was a tiger, sir?" he asked.

A tiger in pidgin means a leopard, a typical example of how animals are wrongly named.

"No, it wasn't a tiger: it was like one, but smaller, and with much smaller mark-mark for his skin."

"Ah, yes, I know this animal," said the Tailor.

"Well, how can we catch it? if there's one up here there must be others, no be so?"

"Na so, sir," he agreed, "what we want is dogs: I know some hunter man near Bakebe who get fine dogs: shall I go send him message to come up?"

"Yes, tell him to come up here to-morrow if he can."

The Tailor went off to arrange this, and I went to see what lunch had been salvaged out of the wreckage of the kitchen.

That afternoon I wandered off alone into the forest, keeping the bulk of N'da Ali on my left so that I would not get lost. I was going nowhere in particular, and so I walked slowly, pausing often to examine the trees and surrounding undergrowth for signs of life. I was watching a huge solitary ant wandering about the leaf-mould, when I heard a rustle of leaves in a tree close by, followed by a loud "tchack! . . . tchack!". A branch dipped gracefully and along it a pair of small squirrels came running, tails streaming out behind them. I realized with delight that they were Black-eared Squirrels, a rather rare forest animal which I had not seen before. With my field-glasses I could see that they were male and female, and apparently engaged in the time-honoured method of flirtation. The female leapt from the end of the slender branch and landed on another some ten feet away, and the male followed her, uttering his sharp cry of "tchack! . . . tchack! . . ." I moved a little closer to the tree so that I could see them more easily, and found that they were now playing a form of hide-and-seek round the trunk. They were delightful little animals to look at: they had orange-coloured heads with a narrow edge of black round their small ears: the upper parts were brindled greenish, and along the sides was a line composed of little white dots. Their tummies were orange-yellow, as were their chests. But it was their tails that captivated me. The top surface was banded faintly with white and black, but the underside was the most vivid shade of orange-red. As they ran along the branches the tail would be held out straight, but when they stopped they would flick it over their backs so that the tip hung down almost on the nose. Then they would sit quite still and flick their tails with an undulating motion for a few seconds at a time, so that the vivid underside gleamed and flickered like a candle flame in a draught. I watched these squirrels leaping and scurrying around that tree for half an hour, bobbing and bowing to each other and flicking their tails among the green leaves, and I have rarely witnessed such enchanting play between two animals. Slowly they played from tree to tree, and I followed them, my field-glasses glued to my eyes. Then, to my annoyance, I stepped on a dry twig: the squirrels froze on a branch and the male cried out again, but instead of being gentle and endearing the cry was now sharp and full of warning. The next minute they were gone, and only a slight movement of leaves showed the place where they had been.

I walked on, considering my luck: in the space of a few hours I had seen a serval and two squirrels, and this was a record for any day. I presumed that, as the mountain was so rarely visited by human beings, the animal population was less suspicious than in the lowlands. Also, of course, the forest here was more open, being broken by cliffs and grassfields, and this made the animals easier to see and approach. As I was musing on this the silence of the forest was suddenly shattered by the most blood-curdling scream, which was followed by bursts of horrible, echoing maniacal laughter, that screeched and gurgled through the trees, and then died to a dreadful whimpering which eventually ceased. I stood frozen in my tracks, and my scalp pricked with fright: I have heard some ghastly sounds at one time and another, but for sheer horrific impact this was hard to beat. It sounded like a magnified recording of a party in a padded cell. After a few minutes' silence I summoned what little courage I possessed and crept through the trees in the direction from which the sounds had come. Suddenly it broke out again, spine-chilling gurgles of laughter interspersed with shrill screams, but it was much farther away now, and I knew that I should not catch up with whatever was producing it. Then suddenly I realized what was making this fearsome noise: it was the evening serenade of a troupe of chimpanzees. I had often heard chimps laugh and scream in captivity, but I had never, until that moment, heard a troupe of them holding a concert in the forest which gave their cries an echoing quality. I defy anyone, even someone who has had experience with chimps, to stand on N'da Ali and listen to these apes at their evening song, without getting a shudder down his spine.

After we had been for some days on N'da Ali I learnt the habits of this crowd of apes. In the early morning they would be high up the mountain screaming and laughing among the tall cliffs; at midday they would be in the thick forest lower down, where they could find shade from the sun, and at this time they were almost silent; in the evening they would descend to the great step along the side of the mountain on which we were camped, and treat us to an evening concert which was prolonged and nerve-shattering. Then, as darkness fell, they would grow silent except for an occasional whimper. Their movement was very regular, and you could tell with reasonable accuracy what time of day it was by listening to hear which part of the forest they were in.

On returning to camp I found that the bird trapper had made the first two captures: one was a Forest robin, which was not exciting as I knew that John had plenty of them, and the other was a drab little bird with a speckled breast, which was almost indistinguishable from an ordinary English thrush. It was, in fact, so uninteresting that I was on the point of letting it go again, but I thought that I would send it down to John for him to look at, so I packed up both birds and sent the carrier post-haste down the mountain to Bakebe, with instructions that he was to be back again early next morning.

The next day he appeared neck and neck with my morning tea, bringing a note from John. From this it transpired that the drab little bird I had sent was, in reality, a Ground Thrush of great rarity, and an important addition to the collection, and my companion exhorted me to get as many as I could. When I remembered how close I had been to releasing what now turned out to be a bird that rejoiced in the name of *Geokichla camerunensis*, my blood ran cold. I hastily called for the bird trapper and informed him that he would get extra pay for each of the Ground Thrushes he procured.

"Masa mean dat bird 'e get red for 'e front?" he inquired.

"No, no, dat one 'e get mark mark for 'e front."

"But", pointed out the bird trapper, with some justification, "Masa done tell me he no want um again."

"Yes, I know. But now I want um . . . plenty plenty, you hear?"

"I hear, sah," said the youth dismally, and wandered off to cogitate on the curious ways of the white man.

As I was eating breakfast the Tailor appeared, and with him was a stocky young man with a lean, intelligent face, and curious pale yellow eyes. At his heels followed a pack of four piebald, lanky, unkempt-looking dogs, with suspicious eyes.

"This is the hunter man, sir," said the Tailor, "he done bring dogs."

After greeting the man, I asked how he hunted with the dogs. For answer he rummaged in the bag that hung from his shoulder and produced four little wooden bells, and these he hung round the necks of his dogs, and as they moved the bells gave out a pleasant "clonking" sound.

"Dis dog", said the hunter, "'e go for bush and 'e go smell de road for de beef and 'e go run quickly quickly. In de bush you no get chance for seeum, but you go hear dis ting make noise and you go follow. So we go catch beef."

It sounded a vague and extremely exhausting process, but I was willing to try anything once.

"All right," I said, "we go for bush and try. . . ."

We set off into the forest, Tailor, Yellow-Eyes, myself, and three others who were laden down with bags and nets, the dogs running ahead of us through the trees sniffing wildly in all directions. For an hour we walked and nothing happened. One of the dogs found some mess or other, and a disgraceful fight broke out as to which of the pack should roll in the delicacy. In the end they shared it, and we proceeded amid a strong and nauseating odour. I was just beginning to wonder if hunting with dogs was all the Tailor had made it out to be, when the smallest of our pack put her nose to the ground, uttered a series of shrill yaps, and rushed headlong into the thickest tangle of undergrowth she could find. The rest of the pack, all giving tongue, followed her, and they were soon out of sight. With a loud cry, which was presumably meant as an encouragement to his dogs, Yellow-Eyes plunged into the tangle of thorns and lianas, and the Tailor and the rest of the retinue followed. Unless I wanted to be left behind it was obvious that I should have to do the same; so, cursing the dog for finding the scent in such an overgrown bit of forest, I pushed my way into the undergrowth, tripping and stumbling, and getting stabbed by thorns and twigs. At last I caught up with the others who were running easily and swiftly, ducking and twisting between the trees and the creepers. Ahead of us the pack was silent except for an occasional yap, but we could hear the little wooden bells clonking like mad.

We ran for what seemed hours and at last came to a gasping and perspiring halt; we listened, between gulps for air, but there was no sound from the dogs, not even the clonking of the bells. Yellow-Eyes gave a few shrill falsetto screeches, but there was no response: we had lost our pack. I lay on the ground, thankful for this respite, filling my lungs with air, and wondering if my heart was going to jump through my ribs. Yellow-Eyes and the Tailor disappeared into the forest, and some time after faint yodels brought us to our feet; when we caught up with them we could hear in the distance the clonking of the bells. We ran on and each moment the sound of the bells grew clearer, and we could hear the dogs yapping frenziedly. We were running downhill now, and the ground was covered with great boulders and fallen trees which made the going more difficult and dangerous. Suddenly we came to a small clearing, and an astonishing sight met my eyes: the dogs were grouped round the base of a small cliff some thirty feet high, its surface speckled with moss and begonias, and, yapping and snarling, they were leaping wildly in the air in an attempt to reach a ledge some ten feet above them, and on it , hissing like a train and lashing with its tail, lay a huge Monitor. Whatever else I thought we should get I had not thought of Monitors, for I had been under the impression that these huge lizards frequented the larger rivers. But there was no mistaking this one for, with its tail, it measured about five feet long. Its great body was raised on its stumpy legs, and its long tapering tail curved ready to strike; its throat swelled with the hissing exhalations of breath, and its long black, forked tongue flicked in and out of its mouth.

It had apparently run up the rock face when pursued, using its long claws to obtain a foothold where no dog could follow. Having reached this narrow ledge it found that the cliff above bulged out, so it could go no further. The dogs were mad with excitement, giving great twisting leaps into the air in an attempt to reach the ledge, frothing at the mouth and yapping loudly. Yellow-Eyes called them off and tied them to a small tree, which they made quiver and bend with their barking and straining. Then we stretched the toughest net we had on to two long poles and, running forward, flung the net over the ledge. As it landed the Monitor leapt forward to meet it, tail lashing, mouth open, and it became intricately entangled in the mesh of the net, and both net and lizard fell to the ground with a crash. We jumped forward, but the reptile was not finished yet, for the net had fallen about him in loose folds, and he had plenty of room to bite and lash with his tail. With some difficulty we got him out of the net, wrapped him in sacks, bound him with cords, and then slung him between two poles. His skin was rough and black, with a scattering of golden spots, pin-head size, here and there; his eyes were a fierce filigree of gold and black. His strong curved claws would have been envied by a large bird of prey. We carried him back to the camp in triumph, and I worked far into the night with the Tailor, fashioning a rough wooden cage out of poles, in which to send him down the mountain to Bakebe.

The next morning, exhilarated and encouraged by the previous day's success, we set off to hunt early in the morning, and the dogs found a fresh scent almost at once. We ran with them for perhaps a mile and then, as before, they were suddenly swallowed in the vastness of the forest, and we could neither see nor hear them. For a long time we wandered around in circles, trying to find trace of them; then I saw Yellow-Eyes cock his head on one side and, listening carefully, I heard the distant purring of a waterfall.

"Eh, sometime they done go for water," panted Yellow-Eyes, "and then we no go hear um."

We ran on, the noise of the falls grew louder, and soon we found ourselves stumbling along the rocky banks of a frothing, tumbling stream. Ahead was the waterfall, a shining wall of water falling from a rock face some fifty feet high into a tumble of big boulders thickly encrusted with green moss and lush plants. Everything was misty with spray, and over the crest of the waterfall hung a tiny blurred rainbow which gleamed and faded with the pulsating of the water. Above the voice of the falls we could now hear the clonking of the bells, and from out of the undergrowth between two rocks backed one of the dogs, stern first, yapping hysterically.

Leaping from rock to rock through the rapids we reached the base of the falls, and clambered eagerly over the slippery rocks to see what it was that the dogs had cornered. There, in a small shady area between the boulders, lay another Monitor, but, in comparison to it, the one we had caught the day before looked like a pygmy. It was curved like a great taut bow, its massive body quite still except for the heaving movement of its ribs. Its mouth was open, and even above the sounds of the waters we could hear it hissing. He had chosen the best place to stand at bay, for on three sides he was protected by rocks, and his claws, tail, and mouth made the other line of attack dangerous to say the least. All the dogs realized this fact except one, a young and foolish bitch, and she had yapped and yarred herself into a fit of hysterical bravery which our presence seemed to increase. Before we could stop her she had rushed into the corner and, more by good luck than anything, had succeeded in fastening her teeth in the loose skin of the Monitor's neck; the reptile, lashing at the dog's thin body with his tail, grasped one of her ears in his sharp-edged mouth. The dog was now in a difficult position, for she could not let go and bound away, held as she was in this vice-like grip. Slowly and carefully the monitor rose on his thick legs and gradually edged his way round until first one and then both of his hind legs were on the unfortunate bitch's back. Then he hunched himself, and suddenly kicked out with his hind feet, raking and tearing the skin off the dog's back with his curved claws. The bitch gave a scream of pain and let go of the reptile's neck, and, to my surprise, the great lizard also released his hold. As she scuttled away from him he lashed round with his tail and bowled her over in a bloodstained heap. She crawled out from among the rocks, shivering and whining, and went and

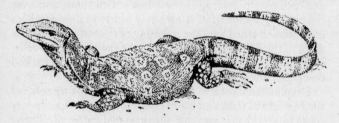

Nile Monitor

sat on the banks of the stream and tried to lick the dreadful wounds on her back. The Monitor was unharmed except for a scratch on his neck, and looked quite ready to give battle again at a moment's notice.

Leaving the Tailor to watch the reptile, Yellow-Eyes and I tied the dogs up to a tree, and I bathed the bitch's wounds. From midway down her back to her rump were seven long gashes, as though she had been sliced with a rather blunt knife. I had just finished with the dog when a cry from the Tailor to the effect that the Monitor was moving sent us all rushing back to the cliff. The reptile had advanced a few yards, but as soon as he saw us he retreated to his corner again. We made several attempts to throw a net over him, but there was no space to manœuvre properly, and the net kept getting caught up on the rocks. There was only one thing to do, and that was to get above him and drop a noose over his head. Leaving the others with instructions to rush in and net him as soon as I had the rope round his neck, I crawled slowly over the rocks to a vantage point above him. I had to move slowly and cautiously for the rocks were slippery with moisture where exposed, and the moss slid off the surface like slime under my feet. At length I reached the small promontory above our quarry and, squatting on my haunches, I fashioned a slip-knot at the end of a long thin cord. Then I lowered it towards the head of the reptile some six feet below me. In my excitement I did not fasten the loose end of the rope to anything, and then added to my stupidity by kneeling on the coil of rope . . . which made my downfall doubly ignominious.

Lowering the noose to within a foot of the lizard's head I flipped it over very neatly and pulled it tight, feeling the rosy glow of pride that goes before a fall. As he felt the noose tighten the Monitor shot forward in a great wiggling dash that jerked the cord from my hands and whipped my knees from under me, so that I toppled over and slid down the rocks, in the most undignified position and with ever-increasing speed. In the brief moment before I landed, with a spine-shattering crash, in the miniature canyon below, I offered up a prayer that my descent would frighten the reptile into the nets. I had no desire to engage him in a wrestling match after seeing what he had done to the dog. Luckily, he was scared and tried to make a dash for it, and his fore quarters were enfolded in a heap of netting. The Tailor and Yellow-Eyes leapt forward on to his lashing tail and hind quarters and pulled the net over completely. As soon as he was well trussed up in sacking and cord I examined the bite on his neck, but I found that the dog's teeth had only just broken the skin.

These two giant lizards were a very welcome addition to the collection, principally because of their size. In the collection at Bakebe I had a number of youngsters, but they were insignificant in comparison. When they are young these

Monitors are slim and neat, their skin a peculiar shade of greeny-black, thickly dotted with groups of bright golden-yellow spots. As they grow older the skin becomes a deep, dusty black, and the yellow spots fade and disappear until only a faint scattering of them remains. They were not difficult feeders, eating anything in the way of dead animals or birds. The things they adored above all else were eggs, and with the use of these delicacies they soon became quite tame, and allowed me to massage their rough backs and pull the dry flakes of skin off when they were sloughing.

When, much later, we returned to camp, I found the traps had yielded a mixed bag of birds, and to my delight it included two of the Ground Thrushes. Although it was so late I felt that the sooner John had these precious birds in his hands the better, so I packed them up and sent them off down the mountain with the Monitor. The carriers moaned and complained at being sent off at that hour, protesting that it would be dark very soon and that the lower slopes of the mountain were notorious for the size and ferocity of its leopards and the cunning and malignancy of its *ju-jus*. So I gave them an extra lantern to ward off these dangers, and watched them out of sight.

Later, while there was still enough light left to see by, I went for a stroll about half a mile from the camp, and presently I found that I was at the edge of a cliff about a hundred feet high. The tops of the trees that grew below were on a level with the top of the cliff, and their lower branches interlaced with the undergrowth growing there. By crawling to the edge of the cliff, in amongst the curling roots and twisted hedge of low growth, I found I was in an excellent position for, being on a level with the massive tree-tops that grew from below, it was as though I had suddenly been transported to the top layer of the forest. I concealed myself beneath a large bush, unhitched my field-glasses and scanned the leaves for a sign of life.

I lay there for a long time, but nothing happened. Faintly, far away down the mountain, I could hear some hornbills honking. Then I heard a faint rustle that seemed to come from somewhere behind me. I had half-turned to see what was making the noise when something landed with a crash of leaves in the bush under which I lay. I lay as still as possible and waited. For a few seconds there was silence, and then from above me came a loud, deep cry: "Oink! . . . Oink!", and I realized that it was a troupe of Mona guenons. For the next half-hour I was treated to the most delightful close-up of monkey life that anyone could wish for.

The monkey in the tree above me was presumably the leader, for he was a male of huge proportions. Having surveyed the forest below the cliff and seen no danger, he had uttered his "all clear" cry to the rest of the troupe, and then he leapt from his bush above me and plummeted downwards like a stone over the edge of the cliff, hands and legs outstretched, to land among the top branches of a tree-top just opposite to where I was lying. He disappeared among the leaves for a few seconds, and then reappeared walking along a branch. When he reached a comfortable fork he seated himself, looked about him, and uttered a few deep grunts.

Immediately the bush above me swayed and shook as another monkey landed in it, and almost in the same movement leapt off again to drop down over the cliff into the tree-top where the old male was waiting. Their progression was very orderly: as one landed in the tree below another would arrive in the bush above me. I counted thirty adults as they jumped, and many of the females had young clinging to their bodies. I could hear these babies giving shrill squeaks, either of fear or delight, as their parents hurtled downwards. When the whole troupe was installed in the tree they spread out and started to feed on a small black fruit that was growing there. They walked along the branches, plucking the fruit and stuffing it into their mouths, continuously glancing around them in the quick nervous way that all monkeys have. Some of the bigger babies had now unhooked themselves from their mother's fur and followed them through the trees uttering their plaintive cries of "Weeek! . . . Weeek!" in shrill, quavering voices. The adults exchanged comments in deep grunts. I saw no fights break out; occasionally a particularly

fine fruit would be snatched by one monkey from the paws
of a smaller individual, but beyond a yarring grunt of indignation from the victim, nothing happened to disturb their
peaceful feeding.

Suddenly there was a great harsh swishing of wind and a
series of wild honking cries as two hornbills flew up from
the forest below, and with the air of drunken imbecility common to their kind crashed to rest among the branches, in the
noisy unbalanced way that is the hornbill's idea of a perfect

Hornbill

landing. They clung to the branches, blinking delightedly
at the Monas from under the great swollen casques that ornamented their heads, like elongated balloons. Then they
hopped crabwise along the branches and plucked the black
fruit with the tips of their beaks most delicately. Then they
would throw back their heads and toss the fruit down their
throats. After each gulp they would squat and stare roguishly
at the monkeys from their great black eyes, fluttering their
heavy eyelashes. The Monas ignored these tattered clowns
with their Cyrano de Bergerac profiles, and continued to feed

quietly. They were used to hornbills, for what the vulture is to the lion, the hornbill is to the monkeys in the Cameroons. Whenever there is a troupe of monkeys feeding, there, sooner or later, you will find some hornbills, giving the whole position away with their loud honking and the swish of their wings, which can be heard a mile away. How the monkeys must have hated the company of these great birds, and yet they had to suffer it.

Presently the hornbills flew off with a great thrashing of wings, and soon after the leader of the Monas decided that it was time they were moving. He grunted a few times, and the mothers clasped their young to their bellies, and then they leapt, one by one, down into the foliage below, and were swallowed up in a sea of leaves. For some little time I could hear their progress through the forest below, the surging crash of leaves as they jumped from tree to tree, sounding like slow heavy breakers on a rocky shore. When I could no longer hear them I rose from my hiding place, cramped and stiff, picked the twigs and the ants from my person, and blundered my way back to camp through the darkening forest.

CHAPTER ELEVEN

The *Ju-Ju* that Worked

The next two days were spent hunting with the dogs, and we had exceptionally good luck. The first day we caught a young Monitor and a full-grown Duiker, but it was on the second day that we secured a real prize. We had spent some hours rushing madly up and down the mountain following the dogs, who were following trails that seemed to lead nowhere, and at length we had halted for a rest among some huge boulders. We squatted on the rocks, gasping and sweating, while our dauntless pack lay at our feet, limp and panting. Soon, when we had all regained our breath somewhat, one of the dogs got up and wandered off into some neighbouring bushes, where we could hear it sniffing around, its bell clonking. Suddenly it let out a wild yelp, and we could hear it rushing off through the bushes; immediately the rest of the pack was galvanized into action and followed quickly with much yelping. We gathered up our things hastily, flung away our half-smoked cigarettes, and followed the pack with all speed. At first the trail led downhill, and we leapt wildly among the boulders and roots as we rushed down the steep incline. At one point there was a flimsy sapling hanging low over our path, and instead of ducking beneath it as the others had done, I brushed it aside with one hand. Immediately a swarm of black dots appeared before my eyes and an agonizing pain spread over my neck and cheek. On the branch which I had so carelessly thrust aside there was hanging a small forest wasps' nest, a thing the size of an apple hanging concealed beneath the leaves. The owners of these nests are swift and angry, and do not hesitate to attack, as I now realized. As I rushed on, clutching my cheek and neck and cursing fluently, it occurred to me that the hunters had seen the nest and had instinctively ducked to avoid disturbing it, and they presumably thought I would do the same. From then on I imitated their actions slavishly, while my head ached and throbbed.

It was the longest chase we had had to date; we must have run for nearly an hour, and towards the end I was so exhausted and in such pain that I did not really care if we cap-

Black-legged Mongoose

tured anything or not. But eventually we caught up with the pack, and we found them grouped around the end of a great hollow tree trunk that stretched across the forest floor. The sight of the animal that crouched snarling gently at the dogs in the mouth of the trunk revived my interest in life immediately; it was the size of an English fox, with a heavy, rather bear-like face, and neat round ears. Its long sinuous body was cream coloured, as were its head and tail. Its slim and delicate legs were chocolate brown. It was a Black-legged Mongoose, probably the rarest of the mongoose family in West Africa. On our arrival this rarity cast us a scornful glance and retreated into the interior of the trunk, and as soon as he had disappeared the dogs regained their courage and flung themselves at the opening and hurled abuse at him, though none of them, I noticed, tried to follow him.

The hunters now noticed for the first time that I had been stung, for my face and neck were swollen, and one eye was half closed in what must have looked like a rather lascivious wink. They stood around me moaning and clicking their fingers with grief, and ejaculating "Sorry, sah!" at intervals, while the Tailor rushed off to a nearby stream and brought me water to wash the stings with. Application of a cold compress eased the pain considerably, and we then set about the task of routing the Mongoose from his stronghold. Luckily the tree was an old one, and under the crust of bark we found the wood dry and easy to cut. We laid nets over the mouth of the trunk, and then at the other end we cut a small hole and in this we laid a fire of green twigs and leaves. This was lit and the Tailor, armed with a great bunch of leaves, fanned it vigorously so that the smoke was blown along the hollow belly of the dead tree. As we added more and more green fuel to the fire, and the smoke became thicker and more pungent, we could hear the Mongoose coughing angrily inside the trunk. Soon it became too much for him, and he shot out into the nets in a cloud of smoke, like a small white cannon-ball from the mouth of a very large cannon. It took us a long time to unwind him, for he had tied himself up most intricately, but at last we got him into a canvas bag, and set off for camp, tired but in high spirits. Even the pain of my wasp stings was forgotten in the warm glow of triumph that enveloped me.

The next morning I awoke feeling wretched: my head ached, and my face was so swollen that I could hardly see out of my copiously watering eyes.

To irritate me still further it turned out to be one of N'da Ali's off days: she had enveloped herself in every available cloud and even the kitchen, a few paces away from the tent, was invisible in the white dampness. As I was gently masticating the remnants of my breakfast, Pious loomed out of the mist, and with him was a short, misshapen, evil-looking man bearing a huge basket on his head.

"Dis man bring beef, sah," said Pious, eyeing my swollen face with disapproval.

The man bobbed and bowed, displaying withered yellow stumps of teeth in his fox's grin. I disliked him on sight, and I disliked him even more on opening his basket and finding inside, not the fine specimen I had hoped for, but a solitary mangy rat with an amputated tail. Having told the man what I thought of his beef I returned to my breakfast. Pious and the man whispered together for a few minutes, the man glancing furtively at me now and then, and Pious came forward once more.

"Excuse me, sah, dis man come from Fineschang, and he say he get something to tell Masa."

The man capered forward, bowing and grinning and flapping his wrinkled hands.

"Masa," he whined, "de people for Fineschang dey angry too much dat Masa done come for dis place. . . ."

"Well?"

"Yesterday dey done put *ju-ju* for Masa. . . ."

"Whar!" yelped Pious, slapping the man on the head so that his dirty hat fell over his eyes. "Na what kind of *ju-ju* dey done put for Masa, ay?"

"No be bad *ju-ju*," said the man hastily, "only Masa no go catch any more beef for dis place, no go get lucky, get plenty rain too much, Masa no go stay."

"Go tell the people of Fineschang I no fear their *ju-ju*," I said wrathfully, "I go stay here until I want to go, you hear? And if I see any Fineschang man for dis place, I get gun that get power too much, you hear, bushman?"

"I hear, sah," said the man, cringing, "but why Masa de shout me, I no get palaver with Masa?"

"My friend, I savvay dis *ju-ju* talk: dis *ju-ju* no fit work if I no know dis ting, and so you be messenger boy, no be so?"

"No, sah, I no get palaver with Masa."

"All right, now you go for Fineschang one time or I go get palaver with you. You hear?"

The man scuttled off through the mist and Pious gazed anxiously after him.

"You want I go beat him, sah?" he asked hopefully.

"No, leave him."

"Eh! I no like dis *ju-ju* business, sah."

"Well, don't tell the others, I don't want them all panicky."

It was the first time that I have had a *ju-ju* put on me, and I was interested to see what would happen. I most emphatically do not dismiss *ju-ju* as a lot of nonsense and mumbo-jumbo, and anyone who does so is a fool, for *ju-ju* is a very real and potent force all over Africa, and has been known to produce results which are difficult to explain away. Perhaps the commonest sort, and the most effective, is where you have the co-operation of your victim. By this I mean that the man must *know* he has had a *ju-ju* placed on him, and then, if he believes in magic, he is ripe for the slaughter. A "well-wisher" comes to the unfortunate man and tells him that a *ju-ju* has been placed on him, and then, if he believes it, he is left in horrid suspense for a time. Slowly the whole plot is unfolded to him by different "well-wishers" (these, in Africa, are just as deadly as their European counterparts) and he learns that he is gradually to waste away and die. If he is sufficiently convinced of the efficacy of the spell, he *will* waste away and die. The man who had just been to see me was one of these "well-wishers", and now that I had been told about the *ju-ju*, it was more or less up to me. The curious thing was that the *ju-ju did* work, better than anyone could have wished, but how much of it was due to my own unconscious efforts, and how much was mere coincidence, I don't know.

The next afternoon, the swelling on my face having gone down, the Tailor, myself, and four others went to the base of some huge cliffs a few miles from camp. These cliffs were riddled with caves, and our object was to try and catch some of the bats that lived in them and to see what else we could find. N'da Ali had recovered from her bad mood, and the day was sparkling with sunlight, and there was even a gentle breeze to keep us cool. I had forgotten all about the *ju-ju* . . . or, at any rate, I thought I had.

To get down to these caves, which were all connected to each other by a network of narrow passages, we had to lower ourselves into a gorge about forty feet deep. We soon found that the ropes we had brought with us were not long enough for this, and so we had to cut great lengths of "bush rope", that thin, tough creeper that grows everywhere in the forest. With these bits of creeper tied together, we lowered ourselves into the gash in the mountain-side. At the bottom we separated, and each squeezed through a different tunnel to explore various sections of the caves. The place was full of bats, from the tiny little insect-eaters to the great heavy fruit-eaters, but for two hours they flicked about us and we caught nothing.

Blundering through the labyrinth I met the Tailor, who was standing gazing at a pile of rocks in one corner of the cave. In an excited whisper he said that he had just seen something move on top of this pile of rocks, high up by the roof. While we were holding a whispered argument as to the best thing to do, we were joined by another member of the hunting brigade, so we all trained our torches on the pile of rocks and surveyed them carefully. There was nothing to be seen.

"Are you *sure* you saw something, Tailor?"

"Yes, sah, sure. 'E dere for on top."

We peered again, and suddenly we were startled by the appearance of a black shape which humped itself above the rocks and grunted loudly.

"Na tiger, sah," said the Tailor.

I was inclined to agree, for the shape was too big to be anything else. On hearing our identification the third member of our little party fled down the cave towards the blessed open air and safety, leaving the Tailor and myself to face the foe.

"Na foolish man, dat," said the Tailor scornfully, but I noticed that the hand that held his torch was none too steady. I was not at all sure what was the best thing to do: if the leopard turned nasty it would be extremely dangerous to shoot at it, for letting off a gun in a cave like that is a dangerous procedure, as it may bring the whole roof down. I felt that I would rather face a live leopard than be buried dead . . . or alive . . . under several tons of rock.

Meanwhile the black shape, after humping itself up several times and giving a few more growls, disappeared behind the rocks, and we heard a faint clatter of rocks. In the shadowy darkness of the cave we could not tell where the animal would next appear, so I was just about to suggest a strategic withdrawal when a head appeared over the top of the pile of rocks, gaped at us for a moment, and then said: "Masa, I done catch beef."

It was the smallest and most useless of the party, one Abo, who had climbed to the top of the rocks in pursuit of a rat. Lying on his stomach he had followed the rodent through the rocks, and the heaving shape we had seen was his backside as he wriggled painfully between the slabs, grunting loudly with the unaccustomed exertion. This anti-climax left both the Tailor and myself weak with laughter, and the Tailor reeled round the cave, tears streaming down his face, slapping his thighs in mirth.

"Eh . . . aehh! Abo, nearly Masa done shoot you. Eh . . . aehh! Abo, you be fine tiger . . ." he chortled.

Abo climbed down from the rocks and held out for my inspection a small rat.

"I tink I done wound him small, Masa," he said, which proved to be an understatement for the rat was very dead.

While we were looking around to see if we could catch any more of these rats, we heard a rumble of thunder from the outside world, which echoed ominously along the caves and passages. When we reached the gorge we found it dark and gloomy, for above us, along the sides of the huge cliffs, swollen black rain clouds were coiling and shifting. We hauled each other out of the gorge as quickly as possible, and started to pack the equipment in the bags. Suddenly the thunder crashed directly overhead, seeming to shake the very foundations of the mountain, and the next minute the clouds swept low over us and an icy sheet of rain descended. I have never seen rain so thick and heavy; almost before we realized what was happening our flimsy clothes were drenched, and our teeth chattering with cold. The sky was scarred by a sudden flash of lightning, followed by a tremendous regurgitation of thunder, and somewhere to our left in the forest I could hear the chimpanzees screaming and hooting a shrill protest at the weather.

The men picked up their bundles and we started off down the hill-side for camp; we had not gone fifty feet when my feet slipped on a rain-soaked rock, and I fell and went bouncing and rolling down the slope, ending up against the trunk of a tree, bruised and scratched with my right leg doubled up under me and hurting badly. For a moment I thought I had broken it until I straightened it out, and then I realized I had only wrenched my ankle. But this was bad enough, for I could not stand on it for the pain. I lay there among the rain-lashed drooping trees, with a shivering group of men about me, trying to rub some life back into my leg. We were a good four miles from camp and my ankle was swelling visibly. It was obvious that we could not stay there indefinitely, and to add to my discomfiture I realized that the storm clouds hanging low over the mountain would bring darkness upon us more quickly than we had anticipated. I sent the Tailor to cut me a sapling, and this he fashioned into a rough crutch. Using this, and with the Tailor supporting me on one side, I managed to hobble along, albeit painfully, and so we progressed slowly through the dripping trees. Soon we reached a more or less level area of forest, and the sound of running water came to us. I was surprised, for the only stream we had crossed on the way up had been a wide shallow one, barely covering our ankles, and yet this one sounded like a well-fed stream. I looked at the Tailor for an explanation.

"Dat small water done fillup," he said.

It was my first experience of how quickly a stream, especially a mountain stream, could "fillup" in a good downpour of rain. The stream we had crossed, shallow as a bird-bath, was now a foaming yellow torrent nearly waist deep, and in this roaring broth, branches, roots, leaves and bruised flowers were swept and whirled among the rocks. The shallowest point to cross was where this stream left the level forest floor and plunged down the steep mountain-side over a great sheet of rock, which had been stripped of its covering of leaf-mould by the waters. The other men went first, and when they were safely across the Tailor and I followed. Slowly we edged our way across, I testing each step with my stick. We reached the centre, and here the force of the water was greatest for it was squeezed between two big rocks. It was here that I placed my stick on a small stone that tilted, my stick was twitched away from my grasp, and I had a momentary glimpse of it sweeping down the slope, bobbing on the surface, before I fell flat on my face in the water.

It was the grip the Tailor had on my arm that prevented me from being swept down the hill-side in company with my stick. As it was, when I landed in the water I felt myself being swept down, until I was brought up with a jerk by the Tailor's hand, but this jerk nearly threw him alongside me into the water. Bent almost double to keep his balance he roared for help, and the others jumped back into the stream and laid hold of whatever bits of my anatomy they could see, and hauled us both to safety. Panting and shivering and sodden, we continued our way to camp.

The last half-mile was the worst, for we had to clamber down the escarpment, crawling from boulder to boulder, until we reached the level strip where the camp awaited us. Only visions of dry clothes, a hot meal and a drink kept me going. But when we reached the camp a dreadful sight met our eyes: the tiny unassuming stream that had whispered and twinkled so modestly twenty feet from my tent, was now a lusty roaring cataract. Swollen with its own power it had burst its tiny banks and leapt upon the camp. The carriers' flimsy huts had been swept away as though they had never existed; half the kitchen was a wreck and the floor knee-deep in water. Only my tent was safe, perched as it was on a slight hillock, but even so the ground under and around it was

soggy and shuddery with water. There was no firewood and
the only means of heating food was the solitary Tilly lamp.
Under these conditions there was only one thing to do: we
all crawled into the tent . . . myself and twelve Africans in a
tent that had originally been designed to accommodate two
at the most! We boiled pints of hot, sweet chocolate over
the lamp, and drank it out of a strange variety of dishes
ranging from tin mugs to animal plates. For three hours we
sat there, while the rain drummed on the taut, damp canvas,
then gradually it died away, and the mountain was enveloped
in great drifts of white cloud. The carriers became busy re-
building their little shelters, and as I watched them I suddenly thought for the first time of the *ju-ju*. Well, the first
round certainly belonged to it: my leg was very bad, and
the rain made everything more difficult, and hunting almost
impossible. I had a bad night, and the next day it rained
solidly and dismally from dawn to nightfall, and my leg
showed no improvement. Reluctantly I came to the con-
clusion that it would be more sensible to call it a day and
give in to the *ju-ju*: down in Bakebe, at least, I could rest my
leg in comfort and be doing some useful work, but sitting up
on top of N'da Ali was not doing anyone any good. So I gave the
orders to pack up and said we would leave the next morning,
whereupon everyone except myself looked very pleased.

The next morning was radiant: as we set off the sun shone
down on us, and there was not a cloud in the sky. A mass of
tiny sandflies, which appeared from nowhere, accompanied
us down biting us unmercifully and, I thought, a little trium-
phantly. When we reached the level forest at the foot of N'da
Ali they disappeared as mysteriously as they had come.

As I hobbled down the road to Bakebe I comforted myself
with the thought that I had, at least, got a few nice specimens
from the mountain. I turned to look at her: in that clear
morning light she seemed so near that you could stretch out
your hand and run your fingers through that thick pelt of
forest. Her cliffs blushed pink and gleaming in the sun, with
here and there on their surfaces a pale, twisting thread of
waterfall, the only sign of the storm.

CHAPTER TWELVE

The Life and Death of Cholmondeley

★

Shortly before we left our hill-top hut at Bakebe and travelled down to our last camp at Kumba, we had to stay with us a most unusual guest in the shape of Cholmondeley, known to his friends as Chumley.

Chumley was a full-grown chimpanzee; his owner, a District Officer, was finding the ape's large size rather awkward, and he wanted to send him to London Zoo as a present, so that he could visit the animal when he was back in England on leave. He wrote asking us if we would mind taking Chumley back with us when we left, and depositing him at his new home in London, and we replied that we would not mind at all. I don't think that either John or myself had the least idea how big Chumley was: I know that I visualized an ape of about three years old, standing about three feet high. I got a rude shock when Chumley moved in.

He arrived in the back of a small van, seated sedately in a huge crate. When the doors of his crate were opened and Chumley stepped out with all the ease and self-confidence of a film star, I was considerably shaken for, standing on his bow legs in a normal slouching chimp position, he came up to my waist, and if he had straightened up, his head would have been on a level with my chest. He had huge arms, and must have measured at least twice my measurements round his hairy chest. Owing to bad tooth growth both sides of his face were swollen out of all proportion, and this gave him a weird pugilistic look. His eyes were small, deep set and intelligent; the top of his head was nearly bald owing, I discovered later, to his habit of sitting and rubbing the palms of his hand backwards across his head, an exercise which seemed to afford him much pleasure and which he persisted in until the top of his skull was quite devoid of hair. This was no young chimp as I had expected, but a veteran of about eight or nine years old, fully mature, strong as a powerful man and, to judge by his expression, with considerable experience of life. Although he was not exactly a nice chimp to look at (I had seen more handsome), he certainly had a terrific personality: it hit you as soon as you set eyes on him. His little eyes looked at you with a great intelligence, and there seemed to be a glitter of ironic laughter in their depths that made one feel uncomfortable.

He stood on the ground and surveyed his surroundings with a shrewd glance, and then he turned to me and held out one of his soft, pink-palmed hands to be shaken, with exactly that bored expression that one sees on the faces of professional hand-shakers. Round his neck was a thick chain, and its length drooped over the tailboard of the lorry and disappeared into the depths of his crate. With an animal of less personality than Chumley, this would have been a sign of his subjugation, of his captivity. But Chumley wore the chain with the superb air of a Lord Mayor; after shaking my hand so professionally, he turned and proceeded to pull the chain, which measured some fifteen feet, out of his crate. He gathered it up carefully into loops, hung it over one hand and proceeded to walk into the hut as if he owned it. Thus, in the first few minutes of arrival, Chumley had made us feel inferior, and had moved in not, we felt, because we wanted it, but because he did. I almost felt I ought to apologize for the mess on the table when he walked in.

He seated himself in a chair, dropped his chain on the floor, and then looked hopefully at me. It was quite obvious that he expected some sort of refreshment after his tiring journey. I roared out to the kitchen for them to make a cup

of tea, for I had been warned that Chumley had a great liking
for the cup that cheers. Leaving him sitting in the chair and
surveying our humble abode with ill-concealed disgust, I
went out to his crate, and in it I found a tin plate and a bat-
tered tin mug of colossal proportions. When I returned to
the hut bearing these Chumley brightened considerably, and
even went so far as to praise me for my intelligence.

"Ooooooo, umph!" he said, and then crossed his legs and
continued his inspection of the hut. I sat down opposite him
and produced a packet of cigarettes. As I was selecting one a
long black arm was stretched across the table, and Chumley
grunted in delight. Wondering what he would do I handed
him a cigarette, and to my astonishment he put it carefully
in the corner of his mouth. I lit my smoke and handed
Chumley the matches thinking that this would fool him. He
opened the box, took out a match, struck it, lit his cigarette,
threw the matches down on the table, crossed his legs again
and lay back in his chair inhaling thankfully, and blowing
clouds of smoke out of his nose. Obviously he had vices in
his make-up of which I had been kept in ignorance.

Just at that moment Pious entered bearing the tray of tea:
the effect on him when he saw me sitting at the table with the
chimp, smoking and apparently exchanging gossip, was considerable.

"Eh . . . eahh!" he gasped, backing away.

"Whar . . . hooo," said Chumley, sighting the tea and
waving one hand madly.

"Na whatee that, sah?" asked Pious, from the doorway.

"This is Chumley," I explained, "he won't hurt you. Put
the tea on the table."

Pious did as he was told and then retreated to the door
again. As I poured tea and milk into Chumley's mug, and
added three tablespoons of sugar, he watched me with a
glittering eye, and made a soft "ooing" noises to himself. I
handed him the mug and he took it carefully in both hands.
There was a moment's confusion when he tried to rid himself of the cigarette, which he found he could not hold as
well as the mug; he solved the problem by placing the

cigarette on the table. Then he tested the tea carefully with one lip stuck out, to see if it was too hot. As it was, he sat there and blew on it until it was the right temperature, and then he drank it down. When he had finished the liquid there still remained the residue of syrupy sugar at the bottom, and as Chumley's motto was obviously waste not want not, he balanced the mug on his nose and kept it there until the last of the sugar had trickled down into his mouth. Then he held it out for a refill.

Chumley's crate was placed at a convenient point about fifty yards from the hut, next to a great gnarled tree stump to which I attached his chain. From here he could get a good view of everything that went on in and around the hut, and as we were working he would shout comments to me and I would reply. That first day he created an uproar, for no sooner had I left him chained up and gone into the hut to do some work, than a frightful upheaval took place among the monkeys. All these were tethered on ropes under a palm leaf shelter just opposite the hut. Chumley, after I had left him, felt bored, so looking around he perceived some sizable rocks lying about within easy reach. Arming himself with these he proceeded to have a little underarm bowling practice. The first I knew of this was when I heard shrill screams and chatterings from the Drills and Guenons, and dashing out I was just in time to see a rock the size of a cabbage land in their midst, fortunately missing them all. If one of these rocks had hit a monkey it would have been squashed flat. Seizing a stick I raced down upon Chumley waving it and shouting at him, trying to appear fearsome, while all the time I was wondering what was going to happen if I tried to deal out punishment to an animal almost my own size and with twice my strength, when I was armed with only a short stick that seemed ridiculously flimsy. However, to my surprise, Chumley saw me coming and promptly lay on the ground, covering his face and his head with his long arms, and proceeded to scream at the top of his voice. I gave him two cuts with the stick across his back, and it had about as much effect as if I had tried to demolish St. Paul's Cathedral with a toothpick. His back was broad and flat, solid muscle as hard as iron.

"You are a very wicked animal," I said sternly, and Chumley, realizing that punishment was apparently over, sat up and started to remove bits of leaf from himself.

"Whoooooo . . ." he said, glancing up at me shyly.

"If you do that again I will have to give you a really good beating," I continued, wondering if anything short of a tree trunk would make any impression on him.

"Arrrrrr . . . oooo," said Chumley. He shifted forward, squatted down and commenced to roll up my trouser leg, and then search my calf for any spots, bits of dirt, or other microscopic blemishes. While he was thus engaged I called the animal staff and had them remove every rock from the vicinity. Later, after giving the beast yet another talking to, I left him, and shortly afterwards I noticed him digging hopefully in the earth near his crate, presumably in search of more rocks.

That night, when I carried Chumley's food and drink of tea out to him, he greeted me with loud "hoo hoos" of delight, and jogged up and down beating his knuckles on the ground. Before he touched his dinner, however, he seized one of my hands in his and carried it to his mouth. With some trepidation I watched as he carefully put one of my fingers between his great teeth and very gently bit it. Then I understood: in the chimpanzee world to place your finger between another ape's teeth and to do the same with his, is a greeting and sign of trust, for to place a finger in such a vulnerable position is a sure display of your belief in the other's friendliness. So Chumley was flattering me by treating me as he would another chimp. Then he set to and soon polished off his meal. When he had finished I sat beside him on the ground, and he went carefully through my pockets and examined everything I had on me.

When I decided that it was time he went to bed he refused to give back a handkerchief which he had removed. He held it behind his back and passed it from one hand to the other as I tried to get it. Then, thinking that the action would settle the matter, he stuffed it hurriedly into his mouth. I realized that if I gave in and let him keep the handkerchief he would think that he could get away with anything, so for half an hour I sat there pleading and cajoling with him, until eventually, very reluctantly, he disgorged it, now very sodden and crumpled. After this I had no trouble with him: if he was playing with something that I wanted I would simply hold out my hand and ask him for it, and he would give it to me without any fuss.

Now, I had known a great number of attractive and charming animals from mice to elephants, but I have never seen one to compare with Chumley for force and charm of personality, or for intelligence. After knowing him for a while you ceased to look upon him as an animal; you regarded him more as a wizard, mischievous, courtly old man, who had, for some reason best known to himself, disguised himself as a chimpanzee. His manners were perfect: he would never grab his food and start guzzling, as the other monkeys did, without first giving you a greeting, and thanking you with a series of his most expressive "hoo hoos". Then he would eat delicately and slowly, pushing those pieces he did not want to the side of his plate with his fingers. His only breach of table manners came at the end of a meal, for then he would seize his empty mug and plate and hurl them as far away as possible.

He had, of course, many habits which made him seem more human, and his smoking was one. He could light his cigarette with matches or a lighter with equal facility, and then he would lie down on the ground on his back, one arm under his head and his legs bent up and crossed, blowing great clouds of smoke into the sky, and occasionally examining the end of his cigarette professionally to see if the ash needed removing. If it did he would perform the operation carefully with one finger-nail. Give him a bottle of lemonade and a glass, and he would pour himself out a drink with all the care and concentration of a world-famous barman mixing a cocktail. He was the only animal I have met that would think of sharing things with you: on many occasions, if I gave

him a bunch of bananas or two or three mangoes, he would
choose one and hold it out to me with an inquiring expression on his face, and he would grunt with satisfaction if I
accepted it and sat down beside him on the ground to eat it.

Chumley had three aversions in life: coloured people,
giant millipedes, and snakes. Natives he would tolerate, and
he got a great kick out of attracting them within range and
then leaping at them with a ferocious scream. Not that I think
he would ever have harmed them; he just liked to watch
them run screaming in fear. But the trouble was that the
natives would tease him if they got the chance, and Chumley
would get more and more excited, his hair would stand on

Giant Millipedes

end, he would sway from side to side swinging his powerful
arms and baring his great teeth, and then Heaven help the
native who came too close.

Giant millipedes fascinated him, but he could never bring
himself to trust them whole-heartedly. The giant millipede
looks not unlike a thin black pudding, with a fringe of legs,
(a hundred or so pairs) arranged along the underside, and a
pair of short feelers in front. They were completely harmless
creatures, that would glide about on their numerous legs,
their feelers waving about, and liked nothing so much as a
really rotten log of wood to feed on. However, their snake-
like motion made them suspect in Chumley's eyes, although

he seemed to realize that they were not snakes. If I placed a couple on his box he would sit and watch them for ages, his lips pursed, occasionally scratching himself. If one walked over the edge of the crate and fell to the ground, and then started to walk in his direction he would leap to his feet, retreat to the end of his chain, and scream loudly until I came and rescued him from the monster.

Snakes, of course, worried him a lot and he would get really most upset if he saw me handling one, uttering plaintive cries and wringing his hands until I had put it down. If I showed him my hands after handling a snake he would always examine them carefully, I presume to make sure I had not been bitten. If, of course, the snake slid towards him he would nearly have a fit, his hair would stand on end, he would moan, and as it got closer, throw bits of grass and twig at it in a vain effort to stop its advance. One night he flatly refused to be shut in his box when it grew dark, a thing he had never done before. When I tried to force him in, thinking he was merely playing up, he led me to the door of the crate and, leaving me there, he retreated, pointing with one hand and "hoo hoooing" loudly and in obvious fear. Investigating his blankets and banana-leaf bed I discovered a small, blind burrowing snake coiled up in the middle. This was a harmless creature, but Chumley was taking no chances.

Not long after Chumley's arrival he suddenly went off his food, lost all his interest in life, and would spend all day crouched in his crate. He would refuse all drink except about half a mug full of water a day. I was away at the time, and John's frantic message brought me hurrying back, for John was not sure what the ape was suffering from, or how ill he really was. On my return I tried everything I knew to tempt Chumley to eat, for he was growing visibly thinner. The staff was sent to search the country-side for ripe mangoes and pawpaws, and delicate fruit salads were concocted with great care by my own hands. But Chumley would not eat. This went on for nearly a week, until I was really beginning to think we should lose him. Every evening I would force him to take a walk with me, but he was so weak that he had to sit down and rest every few yards. But I knew it would be fatal to let him lose all interest in life, for once an ape does that he is doomed. One evening before I went to take Chumley for his walk I opened a tin of Ryvita biscuits and concealed a dozen or so in my pockets. When we had walked some distance Chumley sat down and I sat beside him. As we both examined the view I took a biscuit from my pocket and started to eat it. He watched me; I think he was rather surprised when I did not offer him any, as I usually did, but finished it up and smacked my lips appreciatively. He moved nearer and started to go through my pockets, which was in itself a good sign, for he had not done that since the first day he had been taken ill. He found a biscuit, pulled it out, sniffed it, and then, to my delight, ate it up. He again broached my pocket and got another, which he also ate. Altogether he ate six, and for the next four days he existed on water and Ryvita. Then came the morning when he accepted, first his cup of tea, and then two bananas. I knew he was going to be all right. His appetite came back with a rush, and he ate us out of house and home for about two weeks, and then he returned to normal. I was very glad to have pulled him round, for we were due to leave for Kumba, and he was certainly in no condition to face the journey as thin as he had been.

The day of our departure from Bakebe dawned, and when Chumley saw the lorry arrive to load the collection he realized he was in for one of his favourite sports, a lorry ride. He hooted and yelled and danced on the end of his chain with excitement, and beat a wild tattoo on his crate, making as much noise as possible so that we should not overlook him. When everything else had been loaded his crate was hoisted on board, and then he climbed into it, hooting delightedly. We started off, and we had not gone far before the staff, all clinging to the back and sides of the vehicle, started to sing loudly, as they always did, and presently Chumley joined in with a prolonged and melodious hooting, which convulsed the staff. In fact, the cook-mate found a singing chimpanzee so amusing that he fell off the back of the lorry, and we had to stop and pick him up, covered with dust, but still mirthful. It was a good thing we were not going at any speed.

On arrival at Kumba we had put at our disposal three school-houses belonging to the Basle mission, through the kindness of the Reverend Paul Schibler and his wife. On moving in, as always happened when you made a fresh camp, there was complete chaos for a while, and apart from numerous other things that had to be attended to, there was the question of water supply. While a suitable water-carrier was being employed, furnished with tins, and told to do his job at the double, Chumley made it quite clear that he was very thirsty indeed. He was chained outside, and had already attracted a large crowd of natives who had never seen a fully grown chimp before. In desperation I opened a bottle of beer and gave him that, and to my surprise he greeted its arrival with hoots of joy and smacked his lips over the froth. The lower the level fell in the bottle the more Chumley showed off, and the greater the crowd grew around him. Soon he was turning somersaults, and in between dancing a curious sort of side shuffle and clapping his hands. He was covered with beer froth, and enjoying himself hugely. But this drunken jig caused me a lot of trouble, for it took Chumley several hours to sober up and behave properly, and it took three policemen to disperse the crowd of two hundred odd people who were wedged round our houses, making entry and exit impossible. After that Chumley never had anything stronger than tea or lemonade, no matter how thirsty he became.

It was not long after we settled in at Kumba that Sue arrived. She was the youngest chimp I had ever seen: she could not walk, and was the proud possessor of four teeth only. She arrived in a basket out of which she peered with wide-eyed interest, sucking her left foot. How she had been kept alive by her native owner, who had been feeding her on a diet of mashed coco yam, I don't know. Within an hour she was sucking away at a bottle full of warm milk, liberally laced with sugar and cod-liver oil. When I took her out to show her to Chumley he displayed no interest other than trying to poke her in the eye with his forefinger, so my hopes of a romantic attachment faded.

To any mother who is sick of her squealing red-faced brat I would say, "Go and exchange it for a chimpanzee like Sue: she will be half the trouble and give you just as much pleasure." She spent the night in a warm basket, and the day on my bed, and there was never a murmur out of her. The only time she screamed, clenching her little fists and kicking her legs in gusts of fury, was on those occasions when I showed her the bottle and then discovered it was too hot for her to drink straight away. This was a crime, and Sue would let you know it. She had her first feed at about seven o'clock in the morning, and her last feed at midnight. She would sleep right through the night, a trick that some human babies would do well to adopt. During the day, as I say, she would sprawl on my bed, lying there sucking her thumb or foot, or occasionally doing press-ups on the edge of the bed to get her arm muscles in trim for feeding time. Most of the day, however, she just slept.

Her face, hands, and feet were pink, and she had a thick coat of wiry black hair. On her head this looked as though it had been parted in the middle and then cut in a fringe over her large ears. She reminded me of a solemn-faced Japanese doll. At first sight her tender years (or months) had rather put me off, as I felt that she would require endless attention which I had not the time to give her. But, as it turned out, she was considerably less trouble than any of the other animals. The animal staff were so captivated by her that they would fight for the privilege of giving her a bottle, and I even found John, on more than one occasion, prodding her fat tummy and muttering baby talk at her, when he thought I was not within earshot.

Chumley was, I think, a little jealous of Sue, but he was too much of a gentleman to show it. Not long after her arrival, however, London Zoo's official collector arrived in the Cameroons, and with great regret I handed Chumley over to be transported back to England. I did not see him again for over four months, and then I went to visit him in the sanatorium at Regent's Park. He had a great straw-filled room to live in, and was immensely popular with the sanatorium staff. I did not think that he would recognize me, for when he had last seen me I had been clad in tropical kit and sporting a beard and moustache, and now I was clean-shaven and wearing the garb of a civilized man. But recognize me he did, for he whirled around his room like a dervish when he saw me and then came rushing across to give me his old greeting, gently biting my finger. We sat in the straw and I gave him some sugar I had brought for him, and then we smoked a cigarette together while he removed my shoes and socks and examined my feet and legs to make sure there was nothing wrong with them. Then he took his cigarette butt and carefully put it out in one corner of his room, well away from his straw. When the time came to go, he shook hands with me formally and watched my departure through the crack in the door. Shortly after he was moved to the monkey-house, and so he could receive no more visitors in his private room.

I never saw Chumley again, but I know his history: he became a great television star, going down to Alexandra Palace and doing his act in front of the cameras like an old trouper. Then his teeth started to worry him, and so he was moved from the monkey-house back to the sanatorium to have an operation. One day, feeling bored with life, he broke out and sallied forth across Regent's Park. When he reached the main road he found a bus conveniently at hand, so he swung himself aboard; but his presence caused such horror amongst the occupants of the bus that he got excited and forgot himself so far as to bite someone. If only people would realize that to scream and panic is the best way of provoking an attack from any wild animal. Leaving the bus and its now bloodstained passengers, Chumley walked down the road, made a pass at a lady with a pram (who nearly fainted) and was wandering about to see what else he could do to liven life up for Londoners, when a member of the sanatorium staff arrived on the scene. By now I expect Chumley had realized that civilized people were no decent company for a well-brought-up chimp, so he took his keeper's hand and walked back home. After this he was branded as not safe and sent back to the monkey-house. But he had not finished with publicity yet, for some time later he had to go back to the sanatorium for yet more treatment on his teeth, and he decided to repeat his little escapade.

It was Christmas Eve and Chumley obviously had memories of other and more convivial festivities, probably spent at some club in the depths of Africa. Anyway, he decided that if he had a walk round London on Christmas Eve, season of goodwill, he might run across someone who would offer him a beer. So he broke open his cage and set off once more across Regent's Park. At Gloucester Gate he looked about hopefully for a bus, but there was not one in sight. But there were some cars parked there and Chumley approached them and beat on the doors vigorously, in the hope that the occupants would open up and offer him a lift. Chumley loved a ride in any sort of conveyance. But the foolish humans misconstrued his actions: there he was full of Christmas spirit, asking for a lift, and all they could do was to wind up their windows and yell for help. This, thought Chumley, was a damn poor way to show a fellow the traditional British hospitality. But before he had time to explain his mission to the car owners, a panting posse of keepers arrived, and he was bundled back to the Zoo. Chumley had escaped twice, and they were not going to risk it happening again: from being a fine, intelligent animal, good enough to be displayed on television, he had suddenly become (by reason of his escapades) a fierce and untrustworthy monster, he might escape yet again and bite some worthy citizen, so rather than risk this Chumley was sentenced to death and shot.

CHAPTER THIRTEEN

The Village in the Lake

Kumba was a large village and, for the Cameroons, comparatively civilized: that is to say, it had a white population of about ten people, it could boast of a United Africa Company store and a small hospital, and it was a regular stopping point for all the lorries from the coast. In consequence we thought that it would produce little in the way of rare specimens for us, and we looked on it more as a base within easy reach of port rather than a collecting station of possible value. To our surprise Kumba, and its inhabitants, produced for us some of our very choicest specimens.

The first of these arrived not long after we had settled in the three nice, airy school-houses which were situated on the edge of the village. A wild-looking fellow presented himself one day, bearing on his head a long cage skilfully made out of bamboo, and carefully wrapped in banana leaves. The man, it turned out, was a native from the French Cameroons, some thirty miles away, and he could speak nothing but his own dialect and a sort of pidgin-French. As my French is of much the same variety anyway, I found that we could converse. He told me that he had heard that I was buying monkeys, and so he had gone off to his farm and caught me some. Just like that. He then tore off the banana leaves and displayed to my astonished eyes three monkeys of a species that I had never seen before, sitting in the bamboo cage. On looking closer, moreover, I discovered that there were, in reality, four monkeys, for one of the females clutched a tiny baby to her breast, but it was so small that it was half buried in her fur. They were big handsome beasts, a very dark slate-grey all over, except for two spots of colour: under their chins the hair was soft and fluffy, like a powder-puff, and pure white; on the lower back the hair was a bright rust red in certain lights. Without argument I paid him the very modest price he demanded, and then tried to interrogate him in my very best French. A man who could catch monkeys in this quantity, and of this species, was, I knew, worth cultivating.

Preuss's Guenon

"Allons, mon ami, avec quelles choses avez-vous entrappé ces animaux?" I asked hopefully.

"Pardon, monsieur?"

I repeated, substituting a word for "animaux" that I hoped meant monkey.

The man thought for a long time, scratching his head.

"Je ne comprends pas, monsieur," he said apologetically.

Frantically I looked around for rescue, and at that moment John appeared. Now I knew that my stalwart companion had spent some time in Belgium, and remembered that he could speak French or, at least, had told me that he could. So I called him over and he entered the fray. Speaking with a delightful Oxford accent he translated to my wild tattooed tribesman, and to my surprise the man understood. He replied with a flood of speech, and this time it was John who could not understand. After a hectic half-hour, during which we all spouted French, pidgin, and English at each other, and used nearly every French phrase except "the pen of my aunt", we got the man's story out of him. Apparently he would build a small cage of logs in his farm, somewhere near the place he knew monkeys to be, and then bait it with ripe bananas. When the monkey troupe entered to feast on the fruit they dislodged some sticks, carefully balanced, and the door slammed shut behind them. I implored him to go and catch me more, and underlined it by dashing him two packs of cigarettes. He promised he would try, and left, but I never saw him again. I expect the price he had received for the first lot of monkeys had been enough to keep him going for several months and, according to the Cameroon outlook, why bother to work when you have enough money to buy what you want? Time enough to find a job when you are out of cash. A delightful sentiment, no doubt, and one that displays a very attractive philosophy, but it is hardly the sort of thing a collector wants of his hunters.

The monkeys turned out to be Preuss's Guenon, or the Red-backed Monkey, and a species that had not been seen alive in England for about forty years. As soon as I could I moved them into decent cages, separating the mother and the baby so that they would not be worried or bullied by the others. They were the pride of my monkey collection, and I gloated over them for several days. Then, one frightful morning, some dreadful little child (who I sincerely trust has met with a bad and painful end) crept unseen into the animal house and started to open the cage doors to feed the monkeys. This did not matter with most of them, for they were tame and would accept food from the hand with confidence. But my precious Preuss's had not settled down yet and were certainly not used to strangers opening their cage doors and waving fruit at them. One of the males jumped down and proceeded to bite the hand that was trying to feed him. The boy, of course, leapt back and for a couple of minutes the door was unguarded and open. That was time enough for the monkeys, who were out of their cage and onto the rafters in a second. Just at that moment the animal boys arrived and captured the culprit, saw the monkeys dancing on the rafters, and came running for me. But by the time we had rushed back to the animal house with nets it was too late, and my lovely pair of monkeys were galloping away across the grass in the direction of the nearest trees. The staff gave chase, but they were hopelessly outdistanced. I only hoped that the animals would have the sense to make for the deep forest with all speed, for if they hung around the trees in the village they would most certainly be shot for chop. So now I was left with my solitary female and her baby.

Carefully I approached the cause of my loss whose hand, I noticed with immense satisfaction, was badly bitten. But he glanced at my face, realized that I was not going to be charitable, and fled as fast as his little black legs could carry him. The panting staff returned, and immediately set off in pursuit of the boy, but he, like the monkeys, had too much of a start, and he disappeared among the back streets of the village.

I was still moaning about my loss two days later and hoping that the man from the French Cameroons would return with more of the Guenons, when I received a specimen that more than compensated for the loss of my monkeys. A youth presented himself to me clutching in his arms a box that had once, according to the label, contained bars of Lifebuoy soap. A strong odour argued that it was only recently the soap had been removed from the interior. I prised off the lid and looked into the dark and smelly box, and there crouched an Angwantibo.

Once more there was an uproar: the animal had to be confined in a makeshift cage while a proper one was constructed. The temporary home was not worthy of the beast's rarity and value, but it was better than that suffocating box. The boy was paid, congratulated, and told to try again, which he promised to do. The next day I had just placed the animal in its proper cage, and placed the cage lovingly next to the one that contained the original specimen, when the same boy walked in carrying the same soap box.

"Ah . . . aaa!" I greeted him jovially, "na what beef you done bring? Another same same for dis one?" and I gestured at the Angwantibos.

"Yes, sah," he said unemotionally.

"What?" I said. "You no get same beef again, eh?"

For answer he lifted the lid of the box and displayed a third Angwantibo inside. I could hardly believe my eyes: to get two Angwantibos in two days struck me as being the sort of thing you dream about but never accomplish. Shakily I paid him, told him to try for more, and went to see John about it.

"Guess what I've just got?"

"Something interesting?"

"Another Angwantibo. . . ."

"I say, that's very good," said John, in a pleased tone of voice. "Now we've got three."

"Yes, but what worries me is that I just ask this boy to try for another, and the next day he walks in with one, as though it's no trouble at all. I've just told him to try and get me a fourth. What I will do if he comes back to-morrow with about six of them, I don't know. After all, I can't go on paying that fantastic price."

"Don't worry," said John cheerfully, "I don't expect you will get any more."

As it turned out he was right, but the thought of being confronted with a basketful of Angwantibos at any moment haunted me for several days. I knew I could not have resisted buying them if they had been brought in.

The next good item was a rare and beautiful Superb Sunbird which a small boy brought in, clutched in one hot and sticky hand. Moreover, it was a male, the more colourful of the sexes, and undamaged. I happened to be in the bird house when it arrived and had the pleasure of seeing the usually unemotional John actually gasp with surprise and delight when he saw it. He recovered himself quickly, and became once more the cool and self-possessed Englishman, but there was a feverish glitter in his eye as he bargained with the boy, beating him down mercilessly penny by penny. When he had purchased it he asked the boy how he had caught it.

"With my hand, sah," the boy replied.

"With your hand?"

"Yes, sah, 'e done fly close to me and I done catchum with my hand, so . . ." said the boy, making a fly-swatting gesture with his hand.

John turned to me.

"You are supposed to be the expert on native mentality," he said, "can you tell me why the boys never tell me the truth about catching these birds? To catch this on the wing he would have the eyesight of a hawk and the speed of a rifle bullet. . . . Why does he think I am going to believe such a blatant lie?"

"You look so nice and innocent, old boy, the sort of person that they sell Buckingham Palace to as a rule. There's a sort of shining innocence about you."

John sighed, told the boy to try and get him more birds, and went back to his feeding. But I saw him creep back to gloat over his sunbird later, when he thought I was not looking.

Not long after this the Reverend Paul Schibler asked me if I would like to accompany him and his wife on a trip they were going to make to a village at a lake called Soden, some miles from Kumba. He said, to tempt me, that there were hundreds of birds on the lake, and I would be sure to obtain some nice specimens. I suggested the idea to John and he was very enthusiastic, saying that he would watch over my now considerable collection of mammals and reptiles until I returned. We planned to go for a week, and I prepared a number of small cages and boxes for my captures, rolled up my camp-bed, and set off early one morning in the back of the Schiblers' kit-car, with Pious, who was to minister to my wants. We took the car as far as the road went, and there we collected our carriers and started on our twelve- or fifteen-mile hike to the lake.

Our route was very level and the path wound gently through the forest, in and out of small native farms, and through villages that were mere handfuls of huts scattered about clearings among the great trees. Everywhere the people would come out to greet the Schiblers, shaking hands and calling welcome. Everyone we met stood to one side of the path for us to pass, and would mumble a greeting to us. If they were heavily laden, or suffering from some disease, the Schiblers would pause and inquire after their health or the distance they would have to travel, always ending with the sympathetic "Iseeya". Sometimes we passed beneath bombax trees ablaze with their scarlet flowers, and a quilt of yellow or white convolvulus draped around the base of their great silvery trunks. In the fields the corn husks were heavy and swollen, and their silken tassels waved in the breeze, the bananas hung in great yellow bunches from the trees, look-ing like misshapen chandeliers fashioned out of wax.

It was the evening before we reached the lake. The path twisted like a snake through the trees, and suddenly we stepped out from among the massive trunks and the great expanse of water stretched before us, smooth and grey except where the sinking sun had cast a ladder of glittering golden bars across the surface. The forest ended where the waters began, and all around the lake's almost circular edge its shore was guarded by the trees. In the centre of that vast expanse of water lay a small island, thinly clothed with a scattering of trees, and we could just see the darker mass that denoted the village.

We waded out into the lake up to our thighs in the blood-warm water, and one of the carriers uttered a cry, a shrill, quavering, mournful wail that seemed to roll across the sur-face of the lake and split into a thousand echoes against the trees on the opposite shores. A pair of fishing eagles, vivid black and white, rose from the dead tree in which they had been perched, and flapped their way heavily across the waters towards the island. Presently from the village in the lake, we heard a repetition of the mournful cry, and a tiny black speck detached itself from the island and started across the lake towards us. A canoe. It was followed by another, and then another, like a swarm of tiny black fish shimmering out from beneath a green and mossy rock.

Soon they grounded below us, their prows whispering among the rushes, the canoe-men grinning and calling, "Welcome, Masa, welcome". We loaded our gear into the frail craft, which bucked and shied like skittish horses, and then we were skimming across the lake. The water was warm as I trailed my hand in it and the island, the lake, and the forest encircling them both like a ring, were all bathed in the blurred golden light of a falling sun. The only sounds were the gentle purr of the water along the brown sides of the canoe, the occasional rap of a paddle as it caught woodwork, and the soft grunt from the paddlers each time they thrust their paddles deep into the water, making the canoe leap forward like a fish. Above us the first pair of Grey parrots appeared, with their swift, pigeon-like flight, cooeeing and whistling echoingly as they flew across the golden sky. And so we arrived at the island, almost in silence, a deep calm silence that seemed almost tangible, and any slight noise seemed only to enhance the evening quiet.

The Schiblers had a hut on the crest of the island, in the centre of the village, while I had a tiny shack, half hidden in a small grove of trees, right on the edge of the lake. When I went to bed that night I stood at the edge of the water smoking a last cigarette. The lake was calm and silvery in the moonlight, with here and there a faint dark ring where a fish jumped, plopping the water with a delightful liquid sound. Far in the forest I could hear an owl give a long quavering hoot, and as an undertone to all this there was the distant shimmering cry of the cicadas.

The next morning the light flooded into my shack as the sun lifted itself above the rim of the forest, and the lake looked inviting through my open door. I climbed out from under my net, stepped through the door, and with a run and jump I was in, the waters still warm from yesterday's sun, yet cool enough to be refreshing. I had swum a few yards when I suddenly remembered crocodiles, and I came to a halt and trod water, surveying the lake about me. Round a tiny headland a miniature canoe appeared, paddled by a tiny tot of about five.

"Hoy, my friend," I called, waving one arm, "na crocodile for dis water?"

A peal of shrill childish laughter greeted this remark.

"No, Masa, we no get crocodile for dis water."

"You no get bad beef at all?"

"Atall, sah, atall," said the infant, and I could hear him chuckling as he paddled off across the lake. Thus soothed I enjoyed a long and luxurious swim, and after, ambled up to the village for breakfast. After this I was introduced to two paddlers who were to take me round the edge of the lake to see the birds. They were husky young men, who seemed shy and delightfully quiet, only speaking when spoken to. We set off in a long, deep-bellied canoe, and I perched in the bows, my field-glasses conveniently on my lap, and the gun snuggled alongside mè. Schibler had promised me that I would see a lot of birds, but I had not expected the incredible array we saw that morning.

Round the shallow edge of the lake lay the bleached white trunks of many giant trees, their twisted white branches sticking above the dark waters and casting wiggling, pale, snake-like reflections. These trees had been gradually killed by weather and by insects, and the earth had been softened and washed away from their roots by the lake, until they crashed to their last resting-place in the shallow water, to sink slowly, year by year, into the soft red mud. Whilst their skeletons and their branches stuck above water they provided excellent resting-places for most of the bird life of the area, and as we paddled slowly round the lake I scanned them with my glasses. Commonest of the birds were the Darters or Snake-birds, a bird that looks very like the English cormorant, except that it has a very long neck, which it keeps curved like an S. They sat in rows on the dead trees, their wings stretched out to dry in the sun, their heads twisting on their long necks to watch us as we passed. They were clad in dark brown plumage which from a distance looked black, and gave their upright rows a funereal look, like queues of mutes waiting for the hearse. If we ventured too close they would take wing and flap heavily across the water, and land with much splashing further down the shore. Then they would

Pygmy Kingfishers

dive beneath the water and pop up in the most unexpected places, just their long necks and heads showing above the surface, like swimming snakes. It is this habit of their swimming, with only the head and neck showing, that has earned them the name of Snake-bird.

Next commonest, always sitting in pairs, were the Fishing-Eagles, their black-and-white livery standing out against the green, and their canary-yellow beaks and feet bright in the sun. They would let us approach quite close before flying off with slow flaps to the next tree.

The thing that amazed and delighted me was the incredible quantities of kingfishers of every shape, size and colouring, and so tame they would let the canoe get within six feet of them before flying off. There were Pied kingfishers, vivid black and white, looking from a distance as though they were clad in plumage of black and white diamonds, a domino ready for some avian ball. Their long beaks were coal-black and glittering. There were Giant kingfishers, perched in pairs, with their dark and spiky crests up, their backs mottled with grey and white, and their breasts a rich fox-red. They were as big as wood-pigeons, and had great heavy beaks like knife-blades. There were even some of my favourites, the Pygmy kingfisher, squatting on the more delicate perches, clasping the white wood with their coral-red feet, and among them were the Shining-blue kingfishers, one of the most vivid of them all. These looked not unlike a larger edition of the Pygmys, but when they were in flight there was no mistaking them, for as they skimmed low over the water, twittering their reedy cry, their backs gleamed with a pure and beautiful blue that defies description, so they looked like opals flung glittering across the surface of the lake. I determined, as I watched them, that I would try and take some of these beautiful creatures back to enhance John's collection. The Pygmys he already had, also the rather unlovely Senegal kingfishers, so I made the Pied, the Giant, and especially the Shining-blue, my targets.

Obsessed with this dazzling array of kingfishers I noted all other birds automatically: there were plump, piebald Wattled Plovers, with their yellow wattles dangling absurdly from either side of their beaks, flapping up and down as they trotted to and fro; small glossy Black Crakes, with fragile green legs that trailed behind them as they flew hurriedly from the clumps of reeds; delicate Cattle Egrets, stalking solemnly across the mud-flats; Glossy Ibis like shot silk, peering from the trees with cold and fishy eyes. At one point we came to a place where a tree had only recently fallen, and in falling had dragged with it a great mass of creepers and flowering plants that had been parasites upon it. The still water was littered with green leaves and the bruised petals of the flowers, while among the blooms that still remained, wilting and fading, among the greenery of the trees, a host of sunbirds whirred and fed, sometimes hanging in front of a flower only a few inches above the water, so both bird and flower would have their reflections.

Returning to the village I made inquiries, and soon found three young boys who knew how to make and use the "lubber", or bird-lime, which I had seen used with such success in Eshobi. I told them the type of kingfisher I wanted, and the price I was willing to pay, and left them to it. Very early the next morning, in the pale green dawn-light before the sun rose, I was awakened by the splash of paddles, and looking through the door of my hut I could see three small canoes containing my youthful hunters setting off across the lake. The first one returned about midday, bringing with him a basket containing two Pied kingfishers and one Senegal. The latter I released as John had enough of them, but the Pied I placed carefully in my best cage and gloated over them. They were not, as I had feared, frightened, but on the contrary seemed vastly annoyed. If I placed my hand anywhere near the wire of their cage they would both stab at it with their sharp pointed beaks, and I soon found it was a painful experience to clean out their cages. The feeding problem was easily solved, for the shallows around the island were teeming with fry, and a few casts with nets procured enough for a dozen kingfishers. My pair of Pied fed greedily and then relapsed into somnolence.

In the afternoon the second hunter arrived back with nothing but a Pygmy kingfisher, but the poor mite was so encrusted with "lubber" that it took me half an hour to clean him sufficiently to release him. When I opened my hand he sat for a moment on my finger, grasping it with difficulty in his tiny feet. He settled a few feathers that had become disarranged with the bath I had given him, and then

flew off across the lake, straight as an arrow. The third
hunter returned in the evening, and in his little wicker
basket was a Shining-blue kingfisher. This settled down as
well as the Pied had, but it seemed a trifle more nervous. I
was jubilant, and told my hunters to try for the Giant the
next day. I could imagine John's face if I walked in with
three species of kingfisher for him. But my dream was not
to be realized, for the next day the hunters reported that the
"lubber" was not strong enough to hold the Giant kingfisher.
Apparently, out in the blazing sun, the lime dried up slightly
and, although it was sufficient to hold the smaller birds, one
with the strength of the Giant could easily break away.
However, they did bring me one more Pied and one more
Shining-blue, so with this I had to be content.

That afternoon I was lolling in the warm waters near my
hut and watching the small, fluttering schools of fish investigating my legs, when a man came down from the village
with a message from the Schiblers asking me to go up at once
as a man had brought beef for me. I found a crowd gathered
around what appeared to be, at first glance, a great flattish
stone. Looking closer, however, I saw it was the biggest
freshwater turtle I had ever seen. It was a species known as
the Soft-shelled Turtle: the shell is fairly smooth and domed,
and it protruded round the edge in a great soft rim, like
damp cardboard. The young ones look not unlike thick and
flabby pancakes. The nose of this remarkable reptile is protruded into a pair of miniature trunks, so that the beast can
stick these above the surface of the water and breathe, without displaying any of its body. This unfortunate creature
had been harpooned in the neck, and it expired just as I
arrived on the scene. However, even when its head had been
severed from its body the cruel razor-sharp jaws would snap
a bit of wood and splinter it. I had no idea that these turtles
grew to this enormous size: this one measured four feet in
length, and took two men to lift. After I had examined him
and implored his capturer to get me one alive, the creature
was cut up, and we ate him in a stew. The flesh proved to be
most palatable, like a rich and slightly oily veal. But I never

obtained a live one of these gigantic reptiles, and I was very disappointed.

The day of our departure dawned, we shook hands with

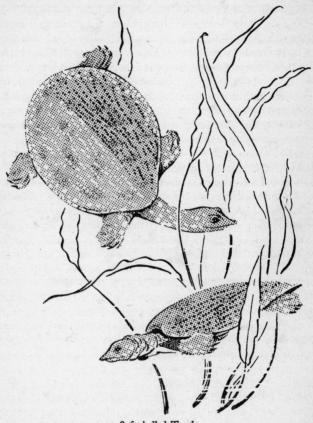

Soft-shelled Turtle

the villagers, paddled across the placid and beautiful lake, and landed on the shore near the path. Before we started I took one last look at the island, lying in the great expanse of sun-shimmering water, ringed with the thick and vivid forest. Then we set off through the trees, and I had to concentrate on watching my carriers to see they did not bump the cages against overhanging branches, or place them in the fierce sun when we rested. Twice I fed the precious kingfishers en route, for I had brought a tin can filled with water, and this contained a mass of tiny fish. One of the Pied kingfishers seemed very wild and would not feed, but the others did not seem to be minding the journey.

In the brief twilight we reached the road, paid off the carriers, and climbed thankfully into the kit-car. It was dark when I arrived back at the school-house and found John just sitting down to dinner. Even John's delight at the kingfishers could not lighten the gloom that I suddenly felt, for I realized that I had just made my last trip. Within ten days we were to leave Africa. I climbed into bed, and as I drifted off to sleep I remembered the warm waters of the lake, the curious little island, the village and its charming and happy inhabitants. One day, I promised myself, I would go back to the village in the lake, just for a holiday. I would swim among the fish and drift alongside the dead trees in a canoe and watch the kingfishers.

CHAPTER FOURTEEN

The Ark Departs

It is easy enough to get a passage on a ship until you explain that most of your luggage consists of a hundred-odd crates of birds, mammals, and reptiles, all very much alive. We had quite a lot of trouble, until the kindness of Elders and Fyffes enabled us to obtain a passage on one of their ships. Once the sailing date was known to us we discovered to our dismay that we had less time to prepare for the voyage than we had anticipated. You cannot just climb aboard a ship with your animals and expect the cook to feed them. There are stores to be bought, meat to be ordered, last-minute repairs to the cages to make sure that nothing will escape on board, and a hundred and one other things. We had to send members of the staff 200 miles upcountry to obtain certain commodities for us which were not grown on the lowlands: ordinary potatoes, for example. At Kumba you could get any amount of sweet potatoes, but no ordinary ones. Then there was corn: when you are buying things in bulk you find it cheaper to buy in the area in which the stuff is grown, and the highlands of the Cameroons are the agricultural areas. We had to have ten dozen eggs, forty stems of bananas in various stages of ripeness, fifty pawpaws, a hundred oranges, twenty pineapples, four sacks of corn, four of sweet potatoes and four of ordinary, two sacks of beans, and the carcase of a whole bullock for meat. All this, as I say, had to be collected from different areas of the Cameroons and brought down to us, and it had to be done quickly if we did not want to sail without some of our precious food-stuffs.

I chose this trying time to go down with malaria. I did not realize it was malaria, but thought I was simply run down, and so I struggled on for nearly a week, feeling like death, until I decided that there must be something the matter with me, and so I paid a visit to the local hospital. The doctor examined me, gave me a huge injection in a most painful part of my anatomy, and ordered me to bed. Very reluctantly I spent two days in bed, while chaos and confusion reigned in the animal house, and John struggled to feed his birds, examine sacks of potatoes, and see that the monkeys were fed. We had decided to travel by night down to the coast, arriving at dawn on the day we were due to get the collection on board and sail. It was the day before we were to start our journey when the doctor called to see me once more. Our hut now resembled a market: there were sacks of food, boxes of eggs, baskets of fruit, all over the floor. The doctor picked his way through this litter, took my temperature, and prepared to give me another injection. While he was holding the needle up to the light and squirting quinine through it (a horrible habit doctors have), and I lay there and quaked, he asked me why there was so much activity.

"Oh, we're leaving to-morrow night," I said cheerfully, eyeing the needle.

"What do you mean, leaving?"

"Leaving to get the ship. We've to be on board by ten-thirty on Tuesday."

"Are you lying there and telling me that you propose to travel down to Tiko and catch a ship to-morrow in your condition?" he rasped. I might have been having a baby from his tone.

"But I'm not so ill," I protested, "I felt fine this morning."

"Listen to me," said the doctor in wrath, "you had a temperature of nearly a hundred and three, on an average, for the last week. You should be kept in bed for at least a fort-night. You can't travel on that ship."

"But I've *got* to, doctor, we had Hell's own job getting

this passage. If we call it off we'll never get another. We've simply got to get that ship."

"You might not reach the ship. In your condition, to take that sort of journey is lunacy: if you had a relapse when you reach the coast (and it's more than likely), you will have to go into hospital, or . . ."

"Or what?" I asked.

"Or die," he said bluntly. And then he jabbed the needle into me with great skill.

As soon as I could speak:

"But we *can't* cancel it now. We've *got* to go."

"All right," said the doctor, "but I won't accept any responsibility for you." And he marched out through the sacks and the baskets and into the night.

The next evening the lorries arrived, the collection was loaded, and then all the food, the sacks of potatoes, corn, beans, the boxes of eggs, and the bullock carcase wrapped in wet sacks to keep it cool. By the time we were ready to start I felt that I was very unpleasantly drunk and my head was throbbing like a drum. I climbed into the cab of my lorry with Sue, the baby chimp, wrapped in a blanket on my knees, and our cavalcade started. It was a nightmare journey, for the first rains of the season had fallen and turned the red earth into a quagmire of sticky clay over which the lorry skidded madly, bumping and jolting over unseen rocks. I could hear the monkeys chattering a frenzied protest from the back of the vehicle and I wondered what rare, and now irreplaceable specimen, would be weakened, perhaps killed, by the jolting. I got some sleep, but it was fitful and uneasy, and once I awoke icy cold and with my teeth chattering, and was forced to stop the lorry and dive into the back to look for blankets to cover myself with. Within ten minutes I was sweating so much I had to unwrap myself once again. At one point we were held up by John's lorry getting a puncture, and John walked down to inquire how I was, and we drank a much needed cup of tea out of the thermos flask.

"How are the birds bearing up?" I asked.

"I don't know," said John gloomily, "we've been over

some frightful bumps. I really daren't look in the back until we reach Tiko."

"I know, I feel the same about mine. Still, we can't do anything until we unload, so let's keep praying."

As we skirted the lower slopes of the Cameroon Mountain and the road dipped towards the sea, a thin cold drizzle started to fall, obscuring still further the landscape that was veiled in the dawn mist. We came to the first of the palm plantations as the rising sun was struggling to shine through the grey clouds that hung low over the mountain. Soon, driving along the edge of the escarpment, we could see stretched below us the great area of flat land that lies around Tiko. This was a bit of civilized Africa, and I shivered as I looked at it: mile upon mile of nothing but banana trees in a great characterless sheet, arranged in neat rows like a green chess-board. Hideous regimentation, a thousand million banana trees standing in serried ranks, obediently bearing fruit that was plucked from them, still green, and carried aboard the waiting ships. Nothing to see but flapping wet banana leaves, like great green shields, sodden and dangling, in endless lines. Occasionally the monotony of this would be broken by a clearing containing a white bungalow, in which lived a European overseer; or a row of horrible corrugated iron sheds, in which lived the banana pickers. Our lorries squelched onwards in the fine drifting rain, and at last came to a standstill alongside a miniature railway. Up and down the tiny track shuffled chuffing engines pulling flat coaches behind them piled high with stems of green bananas. The trains had to cross a swampy area on to the quayside where the ship, with gaping holds, awaited the fruit.

We found, to our dismay, that we had arrived several hours too early, and we could not get the collection aboard for some time; so we left the animals in the lorries, as it was at least a protection from the rain, and there was no sun to make the cages too hot. No sooner had we decided on this than the sun broke through the clouds and shone down on us fiercely, and the rain dwindled and died away. So we set to and unloaded all the crates, piling them in the shade along the side of the train track, peering anxiously into each to make sure its occupant was still all right. When everything was unloaded John and I compared notes.

"I've lost two sunbirds, fortunately not the best ones. I think they were frightened off the perches and just flew around madly, you know, when we went over that very bad bit of road. Everything else seems fairly steady, but I'll be glad to get them on board and feed and water them. How are your things?"

"One Drill's got his hand bashed rather badly, stupid little fool. I think he pushed it through the wire just as we went over a bump, and got it crushed by another crate. But that will heal up O.K., that's my only casualty, thank God. The Angwantibos are all right, but they seem a bit scared."

After a delay that to us seemed interminable, for we could not feed or clean any of our beasts, a train dragging a row of empty carriages drew alongside, and we were told that we could load our crates on it. As we hoisted the last crate on to the train it started to rain again, but not the gentle drifting drizzle that it had been before. No, as we were out in the open and unprotected, the Cameroons decided to show us what she could do in the way of rain. Within seconds all our crates were running with water and the staff, John and myself looked as though we had been dipped in a water tank. Slowly the train jerked its way along the lines, dragging us nearer and nearer to the ship; at last we were alongside, and with all speed the crates were got aboard. I was shivering again and felt like death. Remembering the doctor's warning about a relapse, I hurried down to our cabin and changed into some dry clothes, and then went in search of the chief steward. That understanding man took me into his cabin and poured me out a whisky that could have knocked out a horse, and I felt the warmth of it spreading along my veins. I took some of the tablets the doctor had given me and literally staggered up on deck. Every one of my cages was sopping wet, and the inmates as well. I had to set to and clean each one, scraping out the sodden sawdust and replacing it with dry, and then throwing handfuls of sawdust over the monkeys to try and dry some of the moisture from their dripping fur. Then I made them hot milk and fed them on fruit and bread, for the poor little things were shivering with cold, and I knew that unless I got them dry before nightfall some would most certainly catch pneumonia. After the monkeys I cleaned and fed the Angwantibos, which fortunately had escaped the full force of the rain as they had been sheltered by other crates.

By this time the effects of the whisky had worn off and I began to feel worse and worse. The deck appeared to be heaving and twisting, and my head felt as big as a pumpkin and ready to burst with the pain and throbbing inside it. I began to feel really frightened for the first time: having got on board the ship I did not want to pass out gracefully and be carried off to hospital, leaving John to face the voyage home with two men's work to do. I crawled down to our cabin and flung myself on to the bunk. Presently John came down to tell me that he had more or less got his birds under control, and within half an hour he would be able to give me a hand with the animals, but I had sunk into a deep and restful sleep. When I awoke I felt a different person, and I sallied up on deck still feeling a bit dizzy, but now quite sure that I was not going to die. I finished off the night feed, hung blankets over the front of the monkeys' and the Angwantibos' cages, and then prepared Sue's evening bottle. She screamed lustily when she saw it coming, so the wetting did not appear to have done her any harm. At last everything was done for the night and I could relax, easy in my mind for the first time in two days. I leant on the rail and gazed at the dank and forbidding view of the banana groves and mangrove swamps, and the rain drummed incessantly on the canvas awning above me. Presently John joined me, having completed his tasks, and we smoked in silence, gazing out into the rain.

"I don't think people realize what a job collecting is," said John reflectively, glancing at the dark bulk of his cages, "they don't know the difficulties. Now look at us to-day: we might quite easily have lost the whole collection in that shower of rain. But they never think of that when they see the things in the zoo."

"Well, you can't really expect them to. They think that it's as easy as it apparently was for Noah."

"Noah!" snorted John in disgust. "If Noah had a fifth part of what he was supposed to have carried the Ark would have sunk."

"All those different species of bird and mammals we've seen and collected! If he had only confined himself to what he could get here the Ark would have been overloaded."

"It strikes me", said John, yawning, "that we've got an overloaded Ark on our hands with just the few things we've got." He gestured at our hundred-odd crates.

"Well, I'm going to bed. What time do we sail?"

"About midnight, I think. I'll follow you down in a minute."

John went below, and I stood gazing out into the darkening and rain-striped landscape. Suddenly, between the trees, I saw a small fire spring up, glowing like a red heart in the darkness. Presently, very softly, someone started to play a drum, and I could hear the husky voices of the banana loaders take up the theme. The fire flickered, heart-like, and the drum throbbed, heart-like, in the darkness and the rain. The voices sang softly, chanting a song that was as old as the great forests. A song that was harsh and primitive, yet plaintive and sweet, a song such as the God Pan must have sung. As I watched the pulsing fire among the trees, and heard the beat of the drum merge and tremble with the voices, forming an intricate pattern of sound, I knew that some day I would have to return, or be haunted forever by the beauty and mystery that is Africa.

Finale

The voyage home is not the easiest part of a collecting trip, though one might be inclined to think so. It was fourteen days of extremely hard work for us, but our reward was that we lost only two specimens: one was a bird that had been unwell when we came on the ship, and so its death was no surprise; the second loss was a mongoose which somehow escaped from its cage and, for no apparent reason, walked straight through the rails and into the sea before I could grab it.

I have heard it said that all you have to do is to slip a pound to a member of the crew and then more or less forget your collection until you dock. But even supposing you were to find a member of the crew with that amount of time on his hands (which is unlikely), you would have none of your rarest and most delicate specimens left alive when you arrived, for the man, with all the good will in the world, would not know how to look after them. No, I'm afraid it's not as easy as that. You have to crawl out of your bunk at some unearthly hour of the morning to start the first feed, and from then on there is not a moment of the day that you have free.

Sue was my great problem on the voyage: while in camp she had spent all day sprawled on my bed, getting plenty of fresh air and sunshine. I did not want to keep her closed up in her little wooden cage all the time, yet I was afraid to let her lie on deck for she had just started to crawl, and I did not want her to follow the mongoose through the rails and into the Atlantic. So I had a conference with the chief steward and explained my problem. After some thought he disappeared and returned shortly afterwards carrying a large babies' play-pen. Apparently some lady travelling with her child had left it on board, and I blessed her for this kind if unintentional action. It was duly erected on deck in a nice sheltered position, filled with blankets, and Sue placed within. She thought it was grand fun, and after a few days could stand upright by holding on to the top bar. True, she fell heavily on to her ample bottom each time the ship rolled, but she *could* stand upright for a few seconds at a time, and she felt this was quite an achievement. There was also a delightful arrangement let into the side of the pen: several rows of coloured beads that slid up and down on wire. Sue thought these were marvellous, and would spend hours shooting them up and down, or sucking them hopefully.

The crew, of course, were captivated by her, and they spent all their spare time standing round the play-pen talking to her, or tickling her fat tummy. It was quite ludicrous to see great hairy stokers (who looked as though they had not a pennyweight of sentimentalism in their make-up) leaning over the play-pen and talking baby-talk to a thumb-sucking chimpanzee, reclining at ease on a soft bed of blankets. The day that Sue walked three steps, clutching wildly at the sides of the pen for support, four or five members of the crew, who happened to have been present at this earth-shaking event, came dashing round to tell me about it, as excited as though Sue had been their own joint offspring. I am quite sure that, had I wanted it, I could have had the entire engine-room staff knitting tiny garments for her, such was her hold on them.

The other animals got their fair share of attention as well. Should one of the monkeys develop a cold or a cough the news of this catastrophe would spread through the ship in record time, and soon various members of the crew would be coming up to me with handfuls of sugar or other titbits "for the sick one, mate". The cook and his various assistants always saved the more choice left-overs for their special favourites, and high on this list was, of course, George. He took all this spoiling as a matter of course, and would sit in his cage with a regal expression on his face, accepting whatever was pushed through the bars with a fine air of condescension. Only once during the voyage did he misbehave himself. Sparks, the radio operator, was one of those who always came and talked to George and, so he might better see the baboon in the dim interior of its cage, he would don a massive pair of horn-rimmed glasses. George was captivated by these, and waited his chance to investigate them further. One day Sparks bent too close to the cage and in a second George had reached out and whipped the coveted glasses into his cage. It took me a long time to get him to give them up again, but he had handled them so carefully that when he did return them they were fortunately unbroken.

We were lucky with the weather on the homeward voyage, for it remained calm and fine until we reached the outskirts of the Bay of Biscay; here the sea was leaden and heaving, and a fine cold drizzle fell so we would have known, without being told, that we were approaching England. From our point of view these last few days were the worst, for the temperature dropped and a wild cold wind sprang up and whistled among our cages, making the specimens shiver. If a monkey caught a chill now there was little chance of it recovering. Blankets and tarpaulins were draped over the cage fronts, and the monkeys had hot milk each morning, and again at night. The ship rolled her way round Land's End, the lighthouse blinking encouragingly at us as we gave the midnight feed, and then up the Irish Sea. Then, one dank grey morning we could see the gilded misshapen birds that perch on the top of the Unilever buildings, and we knew that we had reached Liverpool. Our voyage, with all its worries and troubles, was over. Soon would come the greatest joy of all: to see our specimens come out of their cramped cages and stretch themselves after so many months of close confinement.

Unloading your animals from a ship is always a trying business, but at last all the cages were stacked on the docks,

and we could start loading them into the zoo vans. The
Angwantibos, busy trotting through the branches in their
cages, were destined for London Zoo; George, grinning
through the bars of his cage, and Sue, still practising press-
ups in spite of the noise and confusion, together with the
Drills, the Black-legged Mongoose and many of John's
birds, were all going to live down at Paignton Zoo, in
Devon. The Guenons were to take up residence in the new
monkey house at Chester Zoo, and the rest of the creatures
were to be distributed between the zoos at Manchester and
Bristol.

Eventually, the last cage was stowed away, and the vans
bumped their way across the docks through the fine, drifting
rain, carrying the animals away to a new life, and carrying us
towards the preparations for a new trip.

Index

INDEX